Practice Papers for SQA Exams

Higher

Computing

Leckie✕Leckie

Scotland's leading educational publishers

Text © 2009 Ted Hastings
Design and layout © 2009 Leckie & Leckie

02/040810

ISBN 978-1-84372-786-6

Published by
Leckie & Leckie Ltd,
an imprint of HarperCollins*Publishers*
Westerhill Road, Bishopbriggs, Glasgow, G64 2QT
Tel: 0844 576 8126 Fax: 0844 576 8131
leckieandleckie@harpercollins.co.uk   www.leckieandleckie.co.uk

A CIP Catalogue record for this book is available from the British Library.

Questions and answers in this book do not emanate from SQA. All of our entirely new and original Practice Papers have been written by experienced authors working directly for the publisher.

Introduction

Layout of the Book

This book contains practice exam papers, which mirror the actual SQA exam as much as possible. The layout, paper colour and question level are all similar to the actual exam that you will sit, so that you are familiar with what the exam paper will look like.

The answer section is at the back of the book. Each answer contains a worked out answer or solution so that you can see how the right answer has been arrived at. The answers also include practical tips on how to tackle certain types of questions, details of how marks are awarded and advice on just what the examiners will be looking for.

Revision advice is provided in this introductory section of the book, so please read on!

How To Use This Book

The Practice Papers can be used in two main ways:

1. You can complete an entire practice paper as preparation for the final exam. If you would like to use the book in this way, you can either complete the practice paper under exam style conditions by setting yourself a time for each paper and answering it as well as possible without using any references or notes. Alternatively, you can answer the practice paper questions as a revision exercise, using your notes to produce a model answer. Your teacher may mark these for you.

2. You can use the Topic Index on page 6 to find all the questions within the book that deal with a specific topic. This allows you to focus specifically on areas that you particularly want to revise or, if you are mid-way through your course, it lets you practise answering exam-style questions for just those topics that you have studied.

Revision Advice

Work out a revision timetable for each week's work in advance – remember to cover all of your subjects and to leave time for homework and breaks. For example:

Day	6pm–6.45pm	7pm–8pm	8.15pm–9pm	9.15pm–10pm
Monday	Homework	Homework	English revision	Chemistry Revision
Tuesday	Maths Revision	Physics revision	Homework	Free
Wednesday	Computing Revision	Modern Studies Revision	English Revision	French Revision
Thursday	Homework	Maths Revision	Chemistry Revision	Free
Friday	Geography Revision	French Revision	Free	Free
Saturday	Free	Free	Free	Free
Sunday	Modern Studies Revision	Maths Revision	Computing Revision	Homework

Make sure that you have at least one evening free a week to relax, socialise and re-charge your batteries. It also gives your brain a chance to process the information that you have been feeding it all week.

Arrange your study time into one hour or 30 minutes sessions, with a break between sessions e.g. 6pm–7pm, 7.15pm–7.45pm, 8pm–9pm. Try to start studying as early as possible in the evening when your brain is still alert and be aware that the longer you put off starting, the harder it will be to start!

Study a different subject in each session, except for the day before an exam.

Do something different during your breaks between study sessions – have a cup of tea, or listen to some music. Don't let your 15 minutes expanded into 20 or 25 minutes though!

Have your class notes and any textbooks available for your revision to hand as well as plenty of blank paper, a pen, etc. You may like to make keyword sheets like the geography example below:

Keyword	Meaning
Anticyclone	An area of high pressure
Commuters	People who travel into town to work
Erosion	The process of wearing down the landscape

Finally forget or ignore all or some of the advice in this section if you are happy with your present way of studying. Everyone revises differently, so find a way that works for you!

Transfer Your Knowledge

As well as using your class notes and textbooks to revise, these practice papers will also be a useful revision tool as they will help you to get used to answering exam style questions. You may find as you work through the questions that they refer to a case study or an example that you haven't come across before. Don't worry! You should be able to transfer your knowledge of a topic or theme to a new example. The enhanced answer section at the back will demonstrate how to read and interpret the question to identify the topic being examined and how to apply your course knowledge in order to answer the question successfully.

Command Words

In the practice papers and in the exam itself, a number of command words will be used in the questions. These command words are used to show you how you should answer a question – some words indicate that you should write more than others. If you familiarise yourself with these command words, it will help you to structure your answers more effectively.

Command Word	Meaning/Explanation
Name, state, identify, list	Giving a list is acceptable here – as a general rule you will get one mark for each point you give
Suggest	Give more than a list – perhaps a proposal or an idea
Outline	Give a brief description or overview of what you are talking about
Describe	Give more detail than you would in an outline, and use examples where you can
Explain	Discuss why an action has been taken or an outcome reached – what are the reasons and/ or processes behind it.
Justify	Give reasons for your answer, stating why you have taken an action or reached a particular conclusion.
Define	Give the meaning of the term.
Compare	Give the key features of 2 different items or ideas and discuss their similarities and/or their differences.

In the Exam

Watch your time and pace yourself carefully. Work out roughly how much time you can spend on each answer and try to stick to this.

Be clear before the exam what the instructions are likely to be e.g. how many questions you should answer in each section. The practice papers will help you to become familiar with the exam's instructions.

Read the question thoroughly before you begin to answer it – make sure you know exactly what the question is asking you to do. If the question is in sections e.g. 15a, 15b, 15c, etc, make sure that you can answer each section before you start writing.

Plan your answer by jotting down keywords, a mindmap or reminders of the important things to include in your answer. Cross them off as you deal with them and check them before you move on to the next question to make sure that you haven't forgotten anything.

Don't repeat yourself as you will not get any more marks for saying the same thing twice. This also applies to annotated diagrams which will not get you any extra marks if the information is repeated in the written part of your answer.

Give proper explanations. A common error is to give descriptions rather than explanations. If you are asked to explain something, you should be giving reasons. Check your answer to an 'explain' question and make sure that you have used plenty of linking words and phrases such as 'because', 'this means that', 'therefore', 'so', 'so that', 'due to', 'since' and 'the reason is'.

Use the resources provided. Some questions will ask you to 'describe and explain' and provide an example or a case study for you to work from. Make sure that you take any relevant data from these resources.

Good luck!

Topic Index

Computer Systems

					Knowledge for Prelim			Knowledge for SQA exam		
					Have difficulty	Still needs work	OK	Have difficulty	Still needs work	OK
Topic	**Exam A**	**Exam B**	**Exam C**	**Exam D**						
Data representation	1a, 1b, 2, 13b, 13c, 13d	1, 2, 11a, 11b, 11c	1, 2, 13a, 13b	1, 2, 14a, 14b, 14c						
Computer structure	3, 4, 5, 14a, 14b, 14c	3, 11e, 11f	3, 14b, 14c	3, 4, 15a, 15b						
Peripherals	13a, 16e, 16f	4, 11d	4, 14d, 14e, 14f	5, 15c, 15d						
Networking	6a, 6b, 15a, 15b, 15c, 15d	5a, 5b, 12a, 12b, 12c, 12d	5, 6a, 6b, 14a	6, 16a, 16b						
Computer software	7a, 7b, 7c, 16a, 16b, 16c, 16d	6, 12e, 12f	7, 15a, 15b, 15c	7a, 16d						

Software Development

					Knowledge for Prelim			Knowledge for SQA exam		
					Have difficulty	Still needs work	OK	Have difficulty	Still needs work	OK
Topic	**Exam A**	**Exam B**	**Exam C**	**Exam D**						
Software development process	8, 9, 17e	7, 13a, 13b	8, 13c, 13d	9, 16e						
Software development languages and environments	10a, 10b, 17a, 17b, 17c	8, 13c, 13d	9, 13e, 13f, 13g	10, 17						
High level programming language constructs	10b, 11a, 11b, 11c, 17d, 17e, 17f, 18a, 18b	9a, 9b, 14a, 14b, 14c	10a, 10b, 10c, 10d, 11a, 11b, 16a, 16b, 16c, 16d, 16e	11, 12, 17a, 17b						
Standard algorithms	12a, 12b, 17c, 17d	10a, 10b, 15a, 15b, 15c	12a, 12b, 17a, 17b	13a, 13b, 13c, 19						

Artificial Intelligence

| | | | | | Knowledge for Prelim | | | Knowledge for SQA exam | | |
					Have difficulty	Still needs work	OK	Have difficulty	Still needs work	OK
Topic	**Exam A**	**Exam B**	**Exam C**	**Exam D**						
The development of artificial intelligence	19a, 19b, 19c	16a, 16b, 16c, 16d	18a, 18b	20a, 20b, 20c						
Applications and uses of artificial intelligence	20a, 20b, 20c, 20d	17a, 17b, 17c	19a, 19b, 19c, 19d	21a, 21b, 21c						
Search techniques	21a, 21b, 21c	18a,18b, 18c	18c	22a, 22b						
Knowledge representation	22a, 22b, 23b, 23c	19a, 20a, 20b, 20c	20a, 20b, 20c	23a, 23b						

.Computer Networking

| | | | | | Knowledge for Prelim | | | Knowledge for SQA exam | | |
					Have difficulty	Still needs work	OK	Have difficulty	Still needs work	OK
Topic	**Exam A**	**Exam B**	**Exam C**	**Exam D**						
Network protocols	24a, 24b, 24c	21a, 22a, 21b	21a, 21b, 21c	24a, 24b						
Network applications	25a, 25b, 25c, 26a, 26b, 26c, 26d, 26e	22b, 22c, 22d, 24b, 24c	22a, 22b, 22c, 22d	25a, 25b, 25c, 25d, 25e						
Network security	27a, 27b, 27c, 27d, 27e	23a, 23b, 23c	23a, 23b, 23c, 23d, 23e	26a, 26b, 26c, 26d, 26e						
Data transmission	28a, 28b, 28c, 28d, 28e	21c, 21d, 24a	24a, 24b	27a, 27b, 27c						

Multimedia Technology

Topic	Exam A	Exam B	Exam C	Exam D	Knowledge for Prelim			Knowledge for SQA exam		
					Have difficulty	Still needs work	OK	Have difficulty	Still needs work	OK
Development process for multimedia applications	29a, 29b	25a, 25b, 25c	25d	31a						
Bit-mapped graphic data	29c, 29d, 29e, 29f	25a, 25b, 25c	28a, 28b, 28c, 28d	28a, 28b, 28c, 28d						
Digitised sound data	30a, 30b, 30c	26d, 26e, 26f, 26g, 26h	26a, 26b, 26c, 26d, 26e, 26f, 26g	31b, 31c						
Video data	31a, 31b, 31c, 33a, 33b	27a, 27b, 27c	27b, 27c, 27d	29a, 29b, 29c, 29d						
Vector graphics data	31d	28c, 28d	27a	30c, 30d						
Synthesised sound data	30d	28a, 28b	28e, 28f	30a, 30b						
Implications of the use of multimedia technology	32a, 32b, 32c	27d, 27e, 27f	25a, 25b, 25c							

Exam A

Computing   Higher

Practice Papers
For SQA Exams   **Exam A**

Try to answer every question in Section I.

Try to answer every question in Section II.

Select one sub-section from Section III below.

Part A	Artificial Intelligence	Page 16	Questions 19 to 23
Part B	Computer Networking	Page 18	Questions 24 to 28
Part C	Multimedia Technology	Page 20	Questions 29 to 33

For the sub-section you have selected, try to answer every question.

Leckie ✕ Leckie
Scotland's leading educational publishers

SECTION I

Marks

Try to answer every question in Section I.

1. Computers store data internally as sequences of binary digits or bits. In order to interpret a bit sequence we must know which type of data it represents.

   (a) How many bits would be required to represent all the positive integers in the range 0 to 65535?

   1

   (b) What is the effect of increasing the number of bits assigned to the mantissa of a floating-point number?

   1

2. Which method of representing graphics stores images as a list of objects, each with its own attributes?

   1

3. State the function of the *data bus*.

   1

4. Explain the meaning of the term "fetch-execute cycle".

   2

5. Describe **two** current trends in the development of backing storage devices.

   2

6. Computers are increasingly grouped together as networks, rather than operating as standalone machine.

   (a) Define the terms "node" and "channel" as they apply to a computer network.

   2

   (b) State **two** advantages of using switches rather than hubs on a computer network.

   2

7. Computer viruses, which can spread easily from one computer to another, are one of the biggest threats facing network users.

   (a) Which type of computer virus attaches itself to word processor documents, rather than executable files?

   1

   (b) What is the name given to the process by which a virus creates additional copies of itself?

   1

   (c) In what way can a checksum be used to assist in virus detection?

   1

8. Software development is often described as an "iterative process". What does this mean?

   1

9. State the role of the systems analyst in the software development process.

   1

10. Computer programs are normally written in a *high-level programming language* and converted to a machine-understandable form by a *compiler* or *interpreter*.

    (a) What is the most important feature of an *event-driven* language? **1**

    (b) Describe two operations that can be carried out on *character strings* using a high-level programming language. **2**

    (c) What is the principal advantage of using *compiled* programs rather than *interpreted* programs? **1**

11. Computer programs make use of *variables* of various types to store data temporarily.

    (a) What type of data is a *boolean variable* normally used to store? **1**

    (b) A programmer wishes to use a variable to store the weight of an item. Which type of variable would be best-suited to this purpose? **1**

    (c) State two important differences between *local variables* and *global variables*. **2**

12. A computer program is often described as an implementation of an algorithm.

    (a) What is the meaning of the term "standard algorithm"? **2**

    (b) List **three** standard algorithms which often occur in computer programs. **3**

    (30)

[End of Section I]

SECTION II

Try to answer every question in Section II.

13. Diarmid has just taken some photographs of the school sports day with his new digital camera. The photographs are stored on a *flash memory card* as *bit-mapped images*.

    (a) State **two** advantages of storing images on a *flash memory card*. **2**

    (b) In what manner is a bit-mapped image stored? **1**

    (c) The *colour depth* of the images is 24 bits. How many different colours can be represented? **1**

    (d) Each of Diarmid's pictures measures 2048 × 1535 pixels. How much storage space will be required for each picture? Show all working for your calculations. **2**

14. Shona wants a new laptop and has been reading computer magazines to get some idea of the products currently available.

    Marks

(a) She notices frequent references to different types of memory. Explain the function of each of the following types of memory:

    (i) Register   1

    (ii) Cache   1

    (iii) Main memory   1

    (iv) Backing storage   1

(b) Some of the laptops that Shona has looked at have processors with the same clock speed but different amounts of *cache memory*. What effect will this have on the system's performance?   1

(c) Several of the laptops are described as having a *32-bit address bus*. How much memory can be addressed by a *32-bit address bus*?   1

15. Coatbank High School has recently implemented a major upgrade to its computer network. The old network was a peer-to-peer network, but the new one is a client-server network.

(a) State **two** differences between *peer-to-peer* networks and *client-server* networks.   2

(b) The new network allows wireless connections. Give **two** reasons for the trend towards increased use of wireless communications.   2

(c) State **four** advances in hardware or software which have contributed to the increasingly widespread use of networks.   4

(d) The new network offers greatly enhanced security. School staff suspect students of making unauthorised use of computers on the old network to download recordings by their favourite bands. Which **two** laws are the students likely to have broken by doing this?   2

16. Alba Games, a computer games shop located in the West of Scotland, wishes to produce a multimedia catalogue on CD-ROM to promote their product range to potential customers. They need to choose suitable hardware and software for this project.

(a) The company wishes to purchase an applications package which will provide most of the features required to produce their catalogue. What type of package should they purchase?   1

(b) List **three** features you would expect this package to provide.   3

(c) State **two** additional packages the company may need to purchase to supplement the features of the main package.   2

(d) The catalogue will contain a large number of high-resolution photographs. Which graphics file format should these be stored in?   1

The company has examines a range of different models of computer and has finally shortlisted two with the following specifications:

Marks

Feature	Model 1	Model 2
Monitor	21 inch	19 inch
Main Memory	4 GB	2 GB
Cache Memory	2 MB	4 MB
CPU Type	Dual Core	Quad Core
CPU Speed	5.2 GHz	4.8 GHz
Hard Disk Size	600 GB	1 TB
Hard Disk Speed	7200 rpm	5400 rpm
Interfaces	USB2, Firewire	USB2, Parallel
Price	£780	£850

(e) Which model would be best suited to the production of a multimedia catalogue on CD-ROM? Justify your selection in terms of resolution, capacity, speed and cost.

4

(f) Each of the selected models offers a range of interfaces. List two functions of an interface.

2

17. Several different types of language, including procedural languages, event-driven languages and scripting languages can be used to develop software.

(a) State the **two** principal features of programs written in a procedural language.

2

(b) Describe **two** benefits of scripting languages.

2

(c) A user wants to configure a word processing package to create new pages with standard headers and footers. What does she need to do?

2

(d) The days of the week are represented in a computer program by an integer variable named **Day**, which is set to 1 if the day is Monday, 2 if the day is Tuesday and so on, up to 7 if the day is Sunday. A programmer wants to examine this variable and print the word "Monday" if it is equal to 1, Tuesday if it is equal to 2 and so on. Write a short piece of pseudocode showing the most effective way of accomplishing this.

3

(e) Write the pseudocode for a subroutine which will accept three integers as input and return the average of the three numbers. Your pseudocode should show clearly the types of all variables and the parameter-passing mechanisms used.

4

(f) Explain the difference between *value parameters* and *reference parameters*.

2

Marks

18. The usernames for a social networking site are generated by merging the first letter of the user's forename with the first five letters of their surname. For example, Duncan Macdonald would be allocated the username "DMacdo". The usernames are stored in a one-dimensional array of strings. Each user has a unique username.

(a) Write a short piece of pseudocode showing how string operations could be used to generate the username.

4

(b) Write program code showing how this task could be implemented in a high-level programming language which you are familiar with.

2

(c) Write the pseudocode for an algorithm which asks the user to enter a username and searches the array for it. If the username is located, the algorithm should print an appropriate message, giving the username and the location where it was found. If the search ends without the name being found a suitable message should be printed.

3

(d) Modify your algorithm to stop processing once the relevant username has been found.

2

[End of Section II]

(60)

SECTION III

Select one sub-section of Section III.

Part A	Artificial Intelligence	Page 16	Questions 19 to 23
Part B	Computer Networking	Page 18	Questions 24 to 28
Part C	Multimedia Technology	Page 20	Questions 29 to 33

For the sub-section you have selected, try to answer every question.

Part A – Artificial Intelligence

Try to answer every question.

19. Artificial Intelligence has become an increasingly important area of study in recent years. Although recent developments have encouraged this trend, a number of fundamental problems remain unsolved.

(a) What factors make it difficult to produce an accurate and agreed definition of intelligence?

2

(b) In what way has the emphasis in artificial intelligence projects changed in recent years?

2

(c) Describe the effects of **two** different hardware developments on the field of artificial intelligence.

2

Marks

20. The major areas of research in artificial intelligence include Neural Networks and Natural Language Processing (NLP).

(*a*) Describe **four** major components of a neural network.   4

(*b*) Describe **two** ways in which a neural network differs from a human brain.   2

(*c*) Describe **four** aspects of human language that can be the source of difficulties in Natural Language Processing.   4

(*d*) State **two** application areas where Natural Language Processing techniques can usefully be applied.   2

21. A computer program is required to carry out searches on the following search tree:

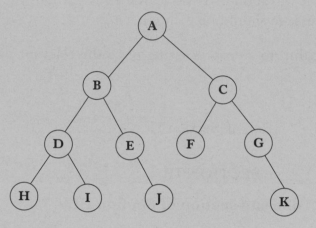

(*a*) In what order would the nodes be visited in

(i) A breadth-first search

(ii) A depth-first search   2

(*b*) In what way do the two search techniques differ in their use of memory?   2

(*c*) In what way can heuristics be used to reduce the time and/or space required for a search?   1

22. Declarative languages are widely used for programming artificial intelligence applications.

(*a*) To what extent is the general software development process applicable to declarative language programming?   5

(*b*) Describe each of the following features of a declarative language, illustrating your answers with examples in a language you are familiar with.

(i) recursion   3

(ii) negation   3

(iii) inheritance   3

23. The following knowledge base describes the relationships between several major Scottish rivers, the tributaries that flow into them, and their final destination.

Marks

```
1.  tributary(clyde, white_cart).
2.  tributary(forth, teith).
3.  tributary(clyde, kelvin).
4.  tributary(forth, allan_water).
5.  tributary(ayr, greenock_water).
6.  tributary(ayr, lugar_water).
7.  tributary(tay, almond).
8.  tributary(tay, earn).
9.  destination(irish_sea, clyde).
10. destination(irish_sea, ayr).
11. destination(north_sea, forth).
12. destination(north_sea, tay).
13. flows_west(X):- tributary(Y, X),destination(irish_sea, Y).
14. flows_east(X):- tributary(Y, X),destination(north_sea, Y).
```

(*a*) What would be the first result of the following query:

```
?flows_east(X).
```
2

(*b*) Trace the first solution to the above query, assuming a depth-first search is carried out. Use the line numbers to refer to specific lines of the program. Your solution should make correct use of the terms *sub-goal*, *backtrack* and *instantiation*.
9

(*c*) What design rule should be followed in when writing Prolog programs to ensure that simple solutions are considered before complex solutions?
2

[End of Section III – Part A]

(50)

SECTION III

Part B – Computer Networking

Try to answer every question.

24. (*a*) The OSI (Open Systems Interconnection) network model breaks networks down into seven layers.

(i) State **two** functions of the Application Layer
2

(ii) Which layer is responsible for end-to-end error recovery and flow control?
1

(*b*) Each computer attached to the internet has its own IP address, allowing it to be uniquely identified.

(i) State the format of an IP address.
1

(ii) Explain why IP addresses are divided into classes.
2

(iii) Describe the structure of a Class C IP address.
2

(iv) Explain how a URL is converted to an IP address.
2

(*c*) Describe the use of each of the following protocols:

(i) TELNET

(ii) SMTP

25. Iain has just been given a new mobile phone which allows internet access.

Marks

(*a*) What protocol do mobile phones and PDAs normally use for internet access?

1

(*b*) State **two** disadvantages of the microbrowsers used on mobile devices compared to normal browsers.

2

(*c*) Describe the format of WML pages.

2

26. Argyll Gifts, a company which manufactures Scottish souvenirs, has decided to sell their products online. After taking advice, they have employed a Search Engine Optimisation (SEO) specialist to ensure that their site is listed by the major search engines.

(*a*) Describe how search engines construct indexes.

2

(*b*) Describe how a web page can be configured by means of HTML tags. Illustrate your answer with an example web page which uses **four** different tags.

5

(*c*) State **two** advantages of e-commerce from the point of view of the consumer.

2

(*d*) One of the company directors is worried about online fraud. What can be done to reduce the incidence of fraud in e-commerce transactions?

2

(*e*) Another director is concerned that some potential customers may be "information-poor". What is the meaning of this term?

1

27. A local company is worried about the security of their computer network and has commissioned you to produce a report on the measures that can be taken to improve security.

(*a*) Describe the steps that can be taken to restrict user access to hardware and data.

2

(*b*) Explain the difference between active and passive attacks.

2

(*c*) Describe **three** different techniques that can be used to carry out a Denial of Service (DoS) attack.

3

(*d*) Describe **two** different methods that can be used to filter the Internet content that users have access to.

2

(*e*) Describe **two** backup strategies that the company could use to restore access to data instantly after a hard disk failure.

2

28. Reliable data transmission is fundamental to computer networks in general and the Internet in particular.

(*a*) Which data transmission method transmits single characters, preceded by one or more start bits and followed by one or more stop bits?

1

(b) Data is generally transmitted over the internet using the TCP/IP protocol suite. List **three** functions carried out by the TCP component of the suite.

Marks
3

(c) Describe two advantages of using *packet switching*, rather than *circuit switching*, in a computer network.

2

(d) A new business user has to choose a dialup, ISDN or ADSL connection. Which of these offers the highest speed and greatest bandwidth?

1

(e) Which type of internet connection would be best suited to a home user who needs good download speeds and wishes to watch television on the same connection?

1

[End of Section III – Part B]

(50)

SECTION III

Part C – Multimedia Technology

Try to answer every question.

29. A company wishes to create a graphically-intensive multimedia application, using images captured with a digital camera.

(a) Does the normal software development process apply to the development of multimedia applications?

1

(b) Describe the use of authoring software to create multimedia applications.

2

(c) Describe the way in which a digital camera uses charged-coupled devices (CCDs) to capture still graphic data.

2

(d) Describe the use of RGB colour codes to represent 24-bit graphics.

2

(e) A digital image is 640×480 pixels in size. What would the file size be if it was saved with a bit-depth of 24 bits? Show all working in your calculations.

2

(f) State the meaning of each of the following image-related terms:

(i) Dithering

1

(ii) Anti-aliasing

1

(iii) Re-sampling

1

30. Stramash Sound is a small company which prepares soundtracks for radio programmes. The soundtracks normally contain a mixture of sounds captured by the company itself and sounds, including MIDI files, obtained from other sources.

(a) Describe the process by which a *sound card* captures audio data, emphasising the role played by the ADC.

4

(b) What is meant by *normalising* a sound file?

2

(c) State the meaning of each of the following audio-related terms: *Marks*

   (i) Clipping 1

   (ii) Stereo 1

   (iii) Surround Sound 1

   (iv) Fade 1

(d) Describe **four** common attributes of notes stored as MIDI data. 4

31. Vivid Videos produces demo videos for up-and-coming rock bands. Their normal approach is to merge footage of the band playing with vector graphic images.

(a) Digital video cameras make use of an array Charge-Coupled Device (CCD) to capture video. Describe the operation of an array CCD. 2

(b) Describe the role of the Analog to Digital Converter (ADC) in a video capture card. 2

(c) Describe the role of the Digital Signal Processor (DSP) in the capture and playback of digital video files. 3

(d) Describe **four** major features of vector graphics formats. 4

32. Recent developments in communications technology have made it much easier to transfer data between devices, using either wired or wireless communication. At the same time, improvements in storage technology have made it easier to store large amounts of data.

(a) State **two** significant differences between *Bluetooth* and *WiFi*. 2

(b) State **two** important differences between *USB* and *Firewire*. 2

(c) In what **two** ways does *holographic storage* differ from other types of optical storage? 2

33. Coatbank Council wishes to produce a Multimedia CD-ROM to promote the town as a tourist destination. The CD-ROM will contain a number of different types of media including audio, video, still images and vector graphics.

(a) Describe **three** items of hardware which will be needed to capture the required data. 3

(b) The council wishes to select a multimedia authoring package which will be used to build the completed product. What facilities will the package need to provide in each of the following areas:

   (i) audio editing 1

   (ii) video capture and editing 1

   (iii) bit-mapped-graphics editing 1

   (iv) vector graphics construction 1

(50)

[End of Section III – Part C]

Computing   Higher

Practice Papers
For SQA Exams

Exam B

Try to answer every question in Section I.

Try to answer every question in Section II.

Select one sub-section from Section III below.

Part A	Artificial Intelligence	Page 30	Questions 16 to 20
Part B	Computer Networking	Page 32	Questions 21 to 24
Part C	Multimedia Technology	Page 33	Questions 25 to 28

For the sub-section you have selected, try to answer every question.

Leckie×Leckie
Scotland's leading educational publishers

SECTION I

Marks

Try to answer every question.

1. What is the decimal value of the unsigned binary integer 110110111101?

   1

2. A radio station needs to digitise 50,000 hours of archive recording. If each hour requires approximately 60 Megabytes of storage, how many 2 Terabyte hard disks will be required to store the digitised recordings?

   2

3. State the functions of **three** registers found in a CPU.

   3

4. State the difference between a parallel interface and a serial interface.

   2

5. A company wishes to replace an old mainframe-based system with a computer network.

   (*a*) State **two** major differences between a mainframe with terminals and a computer network.

   2

   (*b*) State **two** functions of a Network Interface Card (NIC).

   2

6. State **three** reasons why a computer application which runs without problems on one system may not be able to run on another.

   3

7. State **two** reasons why good documentation is essential for a software development project.

   2

8. Explain why it is better to use an interpreter rather than a compiler during program development.

   2

9. A teacher is writing a program to display comments on marks gained by students in an exam. The mark is stored in a string variable named Mark. She wishes to display the word "Excellent" if the mark is A, "Good" if the mark is B and "Poor" if the mark is C.

   (*a*) Using pseudocode, show how this task could be accomplished without making use of if-statements.

   4

   (*b*) Show how this pseudocode could be expressed in a high level language. You can use any high-level language you are familiar with.

   2

10. A company wishes to determine how many of their employees are greater than 1.80 metres in height. The heights of all the employees are stored in a one-dimensional array of real numbers called **height-table**.

    Marks

    (*a*) Which standard algorithm could be adapted to obtain the required information?

    1

    (*b*) Using pseudocode, show how this task could be accomplished.

    4

    (30)

[End of Section I]

SECTION II

Try to answer every question.

11. Coatbank High School has decided to set up a new website and is in the process of carrying out the many tasks involved.

    (*a*) The school has just had a new logo produced, using a vector graphics package. State **two** advantages of having the logo stored in vector graphics format.

    2

    (*b*) The school has an archive of historical photos in printed format. These have been scanned and converted to bit-mapped graphics. Explain why images that are stored as bit-mapped graphics are normally compressed.

    1

    (*c*) All the scanned images have been converted to a standard size of 512 × 384. If the images have a bit depth of 24-bits, how many Kilobytes of storage space will be needed for each image? Show all of your working.

    2

    (*d*) The scanner is connected to the website development workstation by means of a USB-2 interface. Describe **four** functions carried out by an interface.

    4

    (*e*) The school is keen to ensure that the computer system selected for use as a website development workstation is fast enough to carry out the job effectively. Describe **four** different measures of performance that can be used to assess the speed of a computer.

    4

    (*f*) Describe **two** current trends in computer hardware that have made it easier to obtain a powerful computer system for website development.

    2

12. A local company has just installed a new computer network. After due consideration they have decided to adopt a mesh topology.

    (*a*) Draw a labeled diagram showing the components of a computer network with a mesh topology.

    3

    (*b*) State **two** reasons why the mesh topology is more resistant to failure than other network topologies?

    2

    (*c*) Describe **two** advances in computer software that have contributed to the increasingly widespread use of computer networks.

    2

Marks

(*d*) The company intends to store personal information about its clients and employees on the computer network. What legislation must it make sure it complies with?

1

(*e*) The company is very concerned about the possible impact of viruses, worms and trojan horses on its network. Describe how these **three** types of malware differ.

3

(*f*) The company has installed a sophisticated anti-virus package which uses a variety of techniques to detect and eliminate viruses and related threats. Describe **three** different virus detection techniques which could be employed by such a package.

3

13. A company has decided to implement a new Human Resources Management system. The system is based on a proprietary database package and will be written in the scripting language supplied with that package. It has started by producing a software specification and intends to develop the application by using top-down design and stepwise refinement.

(*a*) State the purpose of the software specification.

2

(*b*) State the meaning of the term stepwise refinement.

2

(*c*) Describe **three** distinctive features of a scripting language.

3

(*d*) The company expects to develop parts of the application by using macros. Explain what this means.

3

(*e*) Each employee will be allocated a 10-character employee code consisting of the first five characters of their surname concatenated with the first five characters of their department. For example, if Brian Wilson worked for the Maintenance department, he would be allocated the employee code WilsoMaint. Demonstrate by means of pseudocode how the creation of Employee Codes could be accomplished using the string handling functions of a High-level language.

3

14. A programmer needs a subprogram to calculate the average of ten integer values stored in a 1-dimensional array. Using a high-level language that you are familiar with, show how this task could be accomplished by means of:

(*a*) A subroutine

3

(*b*) A user-defined function

3

(*c*) What is meant by the scope of a variable?

2

15. A meteorologist has the number of hours of sunshine for each day in the month of June stored as a 1-dimensional array of real numbers, consisting of 30 elements. She wishes to determine the minimum number of hours of sunshine that occurred on any day during the month.

Marks

(a) Write the pseudocode for an algorithm which could be used to accomplish this task.

4

(b) Write an implementation of this algorithm in any high-level language with which you are familiar.

4

(c) The meteorologist has now decided that it would be useful to know on which day the lowest number of hours of sunshine occurred. Assume that the data for the 1st of the month is stored in element 1 of the array, the data for the 2nd in element 2 and so on. Describe the modifications to the algorithm that would be needed to obtain this data.

2

[End of Section II]

(60)

SECTION III

Select one sub-section of Section III.

Part A	**Artificial Intelligence**	**Page 30**	**Questions 16 to 20**
Part B	**Computer Networking**	**Page 32**	**Questions 21 to 24**
Part C	**Multimedia Technology**	**Page 33**	**Questions 25 to 28**

For the sub-section you have selected, try to answer every question.

Part A – Artificial Intelligence

Try to answer every question.

16. (a) The Turing Test was originally proposed by Alan Turing in the 1940s as a method for determining the existence of artificial intelligence. Explain why this test is now regarded as inherently flawed.

2

(b) State **two** differences between procedural and declarative programming languages.

2

(c) Describe **two** problems that can arise when applying artificial intelligence techniques in game-playing programs.

2

(d) State **two** advantages of using parallel processing in artificial intelligence projects.

2

17. The Kleenamatic is a home cleaning device which makes advanced use of a number of artificial intelligence techniques. For example, it uses computer vision techniques to recognise objects and expert systems to decide the correct cleaning procedures to be applied in each situation.

(a) Describe the **five** stages of computer vision.

5

(b) State **four** advantages of using expert systems.

(c) Describe **three** other examples of the use of intelligent software to control devices.

3

18. The forenames of all the students in a class have been used to build a binary tree as shown below:

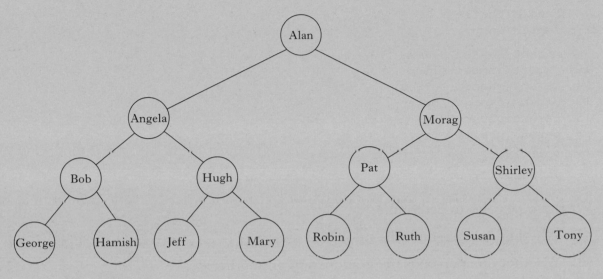

(a) Describe the result of searching the tree and printing out the name encountered at each node using:

(i) A breadth-first search

(ii) A depth-first search

1, 1

(b) State one advantage and one disadvantage of using a breadth-first search rather than a depth-first search.

2

(c) State the meaning of the term "combinatorial explosion".

2

19. A researcher has gathered the following information:

Animals, birds and fish are creatures.
Cats and dogs are animals.
Parrots and canaries are birds.
Trout and goldfish are fish.
Animals travel by walking.
Birds travel by flying.
Fish travel by swimming.
Animals are covered by skin
Birds are covered by feathers.
Fish are covered by scales
Korky is a cat.
Fido is a dog.
Polly is a parrot.
Joey is a canary.
Flipper is a goldfish.
Tammy is a trout.

Draw a semantic net representing this information.

10

20. The following knowledge base describes the relationships between the members of two families over three generations.

Marks

```
1.  male(donald).
2.  male(james).
3.  male(george).
4.  male(peter).
5.  female(sandra).
6.  female(ellen).
7.  female(sheila).
8.  female(mary).

9.  parent(donald, james).
10. parent(james, ellen).
11. parent(sandra, ellen).
12. parent(george, peter).
13. parent(peter, mary).
14. parent(sheila, mary).

15. ancestor(A, B) :- parent(A, B).
16. ancestor(A, B) :- parent(A, X), ancestor(X, B).
```

(*a*) Write a new rules to determine

(i) Whether one person is the mother of another

1

(ii) Whether one person is the grandparent of another

2

(*b*) State be the results of the query:

```
ancestor(george,X).
```

2

(*c*) Trace the trace the steps in the query as far as the second solution, assuming a depth-first search is carried out. Use the line numbers to refer to specific lines of the program. Your solution should make correct use of the terms *sub-goal*, *backtrack* and *instantiation*.

9

(50)

[End of Section III – Part A]

SECTION III

Part B – Computer Networking

Try to answer every question.

21. (*a*) Describe the functions of the Network, Data Link and Physical layers of the OSI network model, indicating the type of device which operates at each layer.

6

(*b*) IP addresses can be subdivided into four classes, A, B, C and D. Describe the function of **each** of these classes.

4

(*c*) Describe **two** different techniques that can be used for error checking in data transmission.

2

(*d*) Describe the operation of the CSMA/CD network control protocol.

3

22. (a) State the function of each of the following protocols: FTP, HTTP, SMTP, TELNET.

Marks

4

(b) Describe the way in which search engines use spiders to construct their indexes.

4

(c) Many people are worried about the ethical implications of the use of computer networks with respect to personal privacy and censorship. Describe current areas of concern for each of these topics.

4

(d) State two of the powers conferred on the Government by the Regulation of Investigatory Powers Act, 2000.

2

23. (a) Describe **three** important reasons for requiring security on computer networks.

3

(b) Describe **four** different techniques that can be used to carry out a denial of service (DoS) attack.

4

(c) Describe **three** different techniques that can be used to restrict user access to computer networks.

3

24. The use of wireless networks and mobile devices is increasing rapidly.

(a) Describe three different types of wireless network.

6

(b) State two disadvantages of using microbrowsers to display data on mobile devices.

2

(c) Describe the use of WML tags to format data for display on mobile devices.

3

(50)

[End of Section III – Part B]

SECTION III

Part C – Multimedia Technology

Try to answer every question.

25. A Graphic Novel publisher has decided that they want to produce downloadable digital versions of all the items in their back catalogue. Each page is to be stored as a single digitised image.

(a) Which graphics file format should be used to store the digitised pages. Why do you think this is the best choice?

2

(b) Each page measures 10" × 8". Pages will be scanned at 200 dpi in 24-bit colour. Calculate how much storage will be required for each scanned page. Show all the working in your calculation.

3

(c) State **four** functions of a Graphics Processing Unit (GPU).

4

26. Kelvin FM is an internet radio station which features music by Scottish bands. The music is streamed as MP3 files.

    Marks

    (a) State the main advantage of using streamed audio rather than embedded audio.

    1

    (b) State the meaning of the term "codec".

    1

    (c) State the meaning of the term "container file".

    1

    (d) Describe **three** techniques used to compress music files to MP3.

    3

    (e) State the meaning of the acronym ADCPM.

    1

    (f) Describe how ACDPM files differ from PCM files.

    2

    (g) Calculate the amount of storage space required for a two-minute stereo file sampled at 44.1 kHz at a bit depth of 16 bits. Show your working in full.

    2

    (h) Describe the role of the DSP component of a sound card in playing audio files.

    2

27. Coatbank Media is a video production company which specialises in the creation of pop videos showing scenes related to the song. They produce their own video footage and match it to the song's audio. The videos are formatted for display on video web sites.

    (a) Describe the techniques used to compress video files from AVI to MPEG format.

    4

    (b) Describe how sound can be added to compressed video files.

    2

    (c) The company's standard format for videos is 320 × 240 pixels, 24-bit colour depth and 30 fps. Calculate how many megabytes of storage will be required for a 3 minute video. Show all working in your calculations.

    2

    (d) Video footage is transferred from the video camera to a PC via a Firewire connection. Explain what advantages this has over USB.

    1

    (e) The company is considering a move in to 3D displays. Explain the difference between real and virtual 3D displays.

    2

    (f) The company currently keeps backups of its videos on DVD, but is considering changing to holographic storage. Describe **two** major advantages this would offer.

    2

28. Coatbank Multimedia has been commissioned to provide background entertainment systems for a chain of hotels. The systems will play MIDI music files while displaying 2D vector graphic images.

    (a) Describe **five** common attributes of notes stored as MIDI data.

    5

    (b) State **two** advantages and **two** disadvantages of storing sound as MIDI data.

    4

    (c) Describe **five** common attributes of 2D vector graphic images.

    5

    (d) State the meaning of the acronyms SVG and VRML.

    2

[End of Section III – Part C]

(50)

Exam C

Computing   Higher

Practice Papers
For SQA Exams   **Exam C**

Try to answer every question in Section I.

Try to answer every question in Section II.

Select one sub-section from Section III below.

For the sub-section you have selected, try to answer every question.

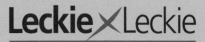
Leckie✕Leckie
Scotland's leading educational publishers

SECTION I

Marks

Try to answer every question.

1. The range of binary numbers that can be stored in a single memory location depends on the number of bits available. State the range of binary integers that can be stored in a 16 bit location.

   1

2. Two's complement form is a common method of representing negative binary integers. Using an 8-bit storage location convert the decimal number -115 to two's complement form. Show all of your working.

   2

3. Several different types of memory can be found inside a computer. State the function of **each** of the following types of memory:

   (*a*) Registers

   (*b*) Cache memory

   (*c*) Main memory

   1, 1, 1

4. Many types of hardware device are continuing to evolve. Describe **two** recent trends in backing storage devices.

   2

5. Although we talk in general of "computer networks" there are various different types of network in existence. State **two** major differences between a LAN and a WAN.

   2

6. There are a number of legal restrictions on the ways in which computers can be used. State which pieces of legislation prohibit the following actions:

   (*a*) Using a computer system without the owner's permission.

   (*b*) Downloading songs and movies.

   1, 1

7. A wide range of different file formats is used for the storage of images on a computer. State **three** standard file formats used for graphics files.

   3

8. Programmers often talk of using "top-down design" and "stepwise refinement". Explain the meaning of these terms.

   2

9. Computer programs are generally written in a high-level language and converted to machine code using a compiler or an interpreter. Explain the principal difference between a compiler and an interpreter.

   2

10. Computer programs make use of various different data types to store different kinds of information. State which data type would be used to store each of the following items of information:

Marks

(*a*) The number of goals scored in a football match   1

(*b*) The distance between two towns   1

(*c*) A telephone number   1

(*d*) The heights of all the students in a class   1

11. Most procedural programming languages provide a range of built-in functions.

(*a*) Explain the meaning of the term "built-in function".   1

(*b*) Describe a built-in function for manipulating strings of characters.   1

12. A teacher wishes to find out if a particular surname is present in a table of student surnames.

(*a*) State which standard algorithm could be adapted to carry out this task.   1

(*b*) Using pseudocode, show how this task could be accomplished.   4

(30)

[End of Section I]

SECTION II

Try to Answer every question.

13. (*a*) Many modern computer systems use Unicode instead of ASCII to represent character data. State the major advantage of using Unicode rather than ASCII.   1

(*b*) Both bit-mapped graphics and vector graphic are widely used for storing images on a computer. State **four** advantages of using vector graphics rather than bit-mapped graphics.   4

(*c*) Software development is often described as an iterative process. Explain the meaning of the term "iterative", giving an example of how it might apply at a particular stage.   2

(*d*) One of the first tasks in the software development process is the production of a software specification. Describe the role of the software specification.   1

(*e*) A variety of different types of programming languages are used for software development. What are the major characteristics of procedural, declarative and event-driven languages?   3

(*f*) State which type of programming language is normally used for writing macros.   1

(g) Many computer programs make use of module libraries. State **one** major advantage of using these.

Marks

1

14. Coatbank Academy has decided to replace its aging computer network with a new one.

(a) The school has decided to use a star topology for the new network. Draw a diagram of this topology, with each component clearly labelled.

3

(b) The school's IT manager is astonished at the range of CPU options currently available. Describe the purpose of each of the following elements of the CPU:

(i) ALU

1

(ii) Control Unit

1

(iii) Data Bus

1

(iv) Address Bus

1

(c) One area in which CPUs can vary is the amount of cache memory available. Describe the impact of cache memory on system performance.

(d) One of the machines on the network will act as a print server. Its main function will be spooling the print jobs sent from other machines. State the meaning of the term "spooling".

2

(e) The printer selected for use on the network can be attached to the server via either a parallel connection or a serial connection. Compare parallel and serial connections, giving one example of each.

4

(f) Students will be able to use their own laptops on the new LAN by means of a wireless connection. State two reasons for the recent increase in the use of wireless communications.

2

15. A friend has asked you to advise her as to what types of utility programs should be installed on her new laptop.

(a) Describe four types of utility programs.

4

(b) Your friend is confused between the different types of malicious programs that could attack her system. Explain the difference between viruses, trojans and worms.

3

(c) Explain why some utility programs might be incompatible with her system.

1

16. A programmer wants to write a program fragment which will accept the number of the current month and print it out as a word, for example, if the number of the month is 1 it will print "January".

(a) Write pseudocode showing how this could be achieved without the use of if statements. (There is no need to show the pseudocode for all twelve months – the first and last will be sufficient.)

3

(b) Implement your pseudocode as a procedure or subroutine in any high-level programming language you are familiar with.

Marks

3

(c) State the difference between procedures/subroutines and user-defined functions.

2

(d) Explain why modularity is important in program design.

2

(e) Describe the difference between call by reference and call by value when passing data to subprograms.

2

17. A climatologist has the rainfall for each day in a month stored in an array of integers.

(a) Write the pseudocode for an algorithm to find the day with the highest rainfall and print both the highest rainfall and the day on which it occurred. Assume for the moment that the rainfall on each day is different.

5

(b) State what would happen if the same level of rainfall could occur on more than one day. What changes would be needed to your algorithm to print the numbers of all the days on which the highest rainfall occurred?

5

[End of Section II]

(60)

SECTION III

Marks

Select one sub-section of Section III.

Part A   **Artificial Intelligence**   **Page 44**   **Questions 18 to 20**
Part B   **Computer Networking**   **Page 46**   **Questions 21 to 24**
Part C   **Multimedia Technology**   **Page 47**   **Questions 25 to 26**

For the sub-section you have selected, try to answer every question.

Part A – Artificial Intelligence

Try to answer every question.

18. (*a*) It is difficult to produce an accurate and agreed definition of intelligence, but fortunately there is general agreement on what constitutes intelligent behaviour. Describe **four** important characteristics of intelligent behaviour.   **4**

(*b*) Artificial intelligence techniques have been used for many years in game-playing programs, particularly for board games such as chess. Describe **four** difficulties that can arise in developing AI programs to play games.   **4**

(*c*) Many AI applications involve searching trees. Searches can be carried out breadth-first or depth-first. Explain the difference between these **two** searching techniques with reference to:

  (i) order of visiting nodes

  (ii) memory requirements

  (iii) backtracking

Illustrate your answer with a diagram.   **5**

19. (*a*) Neural nets are an important area of study in AI. Describe the way in which learning takes place in a neural net.   **2**

(*b*) Describe **two** different ways in which a neural net can be implemented.   **2**

(*c*) Describe **four** important applications of Natural Language Processing (NLP).   **4**

(*d*) Many practical problems can be encountered when constructing intelligent robots. Describe **two** of these problems and the strategies used to overcome them.   **4**

20. Declarative languages implement a number of features which are not found in procedural languages.

Marks

(*a*) Describe each of the following features, giving examples in Prolog or a similar declarative language:

    (i) Multi-argument clauses   2

    (ii) Recursive rules   2

    (iii) Multiple-variable queries   2

    (iv) Negation   2

    (v) Inheritance   2

(*b*) Explain the meaning of each of the following terms as applied to the execution of a query in Prolog or a similar declarative language:

    (i) Goal   2

    (ii) Sub-goal   2

    (iii) Instantiation   2

    (iv) Matching   2

(*c*) The following knowledge base shows the computing habits of a number of users:

```
1.  uses_facebook(john).
2.  uses_facebook(anne).
3.  uses_twitter(michael).
4.  uses_twitter(susan).
5.  uses_wordpress(anne).
6.  uses_wordpress(john).
7.  uses_moveabletype(george).
8.  uses_moveabletype(michael).
9.  plays_gta(anne).
10. plays_gta(margaret).
11. plays_halo(george).
12. plays_halo(john).

13. socialiser(X) :- uses_facebook(X); uses_twitter(X).
14. blogger(X) :- uses_wordpress(X); uses_moveabletype(X).
15. gamer(X) :- plays_gta(X); plays_halo(X).

16. geek(X) :- socialiser(X), blogger(X), gamer(X).
```

    (i) What would be the output of the following query:

       `blogger(X).`   2

    (ii) Trace the execution of the following query as far as the first result:

       `geek(X).`   5

[End of Section III – Part A]   **(50)**

SECTION III

Marks

Part B – Computer Networking

Try to answer every question.

21. (*a*) Describe the functions of the top four layers (Application, Presentation, and Session and Transport Layers) of the OSI Network model.

8

(*b*) A variety of different protocols are use in computer networks. Fill in the blanks (either Protocol Name or Function) in the following table.

Protocol Name	Function
	Logging on remotely to a server.
HTTP	
	Uploading and downloading files from a server
SMTP	

1, 1, 1, 1

(*c*) Describe the function of the Domain Name Service (DNS).

22. "Gadgets Galore" is a new company which has been set up to sell consumer electronics devices online. The following text is extracted from a prototype of the company's new web site:

```
<html>

<head>
<title> Gadgets Galore </title>
</head>

<body bgcolor="white" text="blue">

<h1> Welcome to Gadgets Galore </h1>

<p> Gadgets Galore is your online source for smartphones,
MP3 players, games consoles, netbooks and all sorts of
other consumer electronics devices. </p>

</body>

</html>
```

(*a*) Explain the function of **two** of the HTML tags used in this extract.

4

(*b*) Gadgets Galore will function solely as an e-commerce store. State **three** advantages and **three** disadvantages of e-commerce.

6

(*c*) One of the great areas of consumer concern about e-commerce is the possibility of fraud. Describe **two** steps that can be taken to minimise the incidence of fraud.

4

(*d*) Describe the effect that increased use of e-commerce is likely to have on employment.

3

Marks

23. An online insurance broker has just suffered a major denial of service (DoS) attack.

(a) Describe the impact that this attack is likely to have on the company's customers.

2

(b) Explain the costs the company is likely to incur in combating and recovering from this attack.

2

(c) Explain why someone might want to mount a DoS attack on a company.

2

(d) Describe **three** ways in which the use of a firewall could help protect the company from further attacks.

3

(e) Describe **two** backup strategies the company could adopt in order to ensure a speedy recovery from any future attack?

2

24. (a) The TCP/IP protocol suite is fundamental to the operation of the Internet. Describe the process of transmitting data over a network using TCP/IP, distinguishing clearly between the functions of TCP and IP.

6

(b) Describe **two** functions carried out by a network interface card (NIC).

2

(50)

[End of Section III – Part B]

SECTION III

Part C – Multimedia Technology

Try to answer every question.

25. Multimedia applications play an increasingly large role in our everyday lives, largely due to the technological developments which have made them affordable.

(a) Describe **two** common uses of Bluetooth technology.

2

(b) Describe **two** ways in which holographic storage differs from other types of optical storage.

2

(c) Explain the difference between real and virtual 3D displays.

2

(d) State **two** advantages of using streaming data rather than embedded files in web-based applications.

2

26. MP3 has become an increasingly important format for the storage and delivery of digitised music.

(a) Describe the techniques used to convert analogue audio to MP3.

3

(b) Explain why MP3 is described as a "lossy" format.

1

(c) What is the meaning of the tem "bit-rate" as applied to audio files?

1

(d) State the name given to the process of ensuring that all the tracks on a digitised album will play at a similar volume level?

Marks

1

(e) Describe the difference between "stereo" and "surround sound".

2

(f) Explain what happens when the volume level of an input sound signal is too high for the sound card to deal with.

1

(g) State the name given to the technique of gradually decreasing the volume towards the end of a track.

1

27. "Techno Titles" is a company which specialises in producing attractive title sequences for music videos. The tiles are generated using a vector graphics package before being incorporated into the video files.

(a) Describe the **four** main features of the vector graphics format.

4

(b) Describe **three** techniques used for the compression of video files.

3

(c) Explain how sound can be incorporated into digital video files.

2

(d) State the meaning of each of the following terms as applied to video editing software:

(i) Timeline

(ii) Transition

(iii) Sequencing

1, 1, 1

28. A comics publisher has decided to repackage some of their material as video slideshows accompanied by a MIDI backing track. Each panel in a comic will be scanned as a separate frame and displayed for a few seconds before moving on to the next panel. A high-end scanner will be used to scan the panels.

(a) Describe how a scanner operates, with particular emphasis on the roles of the linear CCD and the ADC.

4

(b) A typical panel measures 4" × 3". If the panels are scanned at 200 dpi using 24-bit colour, calculate how much storage will be required for each panel. Show all the working in your calculation.

3

(c) Explain the difference between anti-aliasing and dithering.

2

(d) State the meaning of the term "re-sampling".

2

(e) State **two** advantages and two disadvantages of storing sound as MIDI data.

4

(f) Describe **five** common attributes of notes stored as MIDI data.

5

[End of Section III – Part C]

(50)

Exam D

Computing   Higher

Practice Papers
For SQA Exams   **Exam D**

Try to answer every question in Section I.

Try to answer every question in Section II.

Select one sub-section from Section III below.

Part A	Artificial Intelligence	Page 55	Questions 20 to 23
Part B	Computer Networking	Page 57	Questions 24 to 27
Part C	Multimedia Technology	Page 59	Questions 28 to 31

For the sub-section you have selected, try to answer every question.

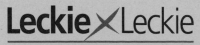
Leckie × Leckie
Scotland's leading educational publishers

SECTION I

Marks

Try to answer every question.

1. Signed binary integers are often represented in two's complement form. Show how the decimal number -103 would be represented in two's complement form in an 8-bit storage location. Show all of your working.

   2

2. State the effect of increasing the number of bits assigned to the exponent of a floating point number.

   1

3. State the function of each of the following components of a processor:

   (i) the ALU

   (ii) the control unit

   1, 1

4. State which line in the control bus stops the execution of the current program and initiates a reboot.

   1

5. State **two** advantages of solid state memory devices.

   2

6. (*a*) Describe **two** major advantages of client-server networks as compared to peer-to-peer networks.

   2

   (*b*) State the functions of two different types of servers that you might find attached to a computer network.

   2

7. State the function of a bootstrap loader.

   1

8. State **two** differences between a trojan horse and an ordinary computer virus.

   2

9. Describe the role of a computer programmer in the software development process?

   2

10. State **two** common uses of scripting languages.

   2

11. State which data type would be most suitable for storing each of the following items about employees in a computer program for processing personnel data:

   (i) Surname

   1

   (ii) Gender

   1

   (iii) Number of Dependents

   1

   (iv) Height

   1

Marks

12. Describe **two** string-handling functions normally provided by high-level programming languages.

2

13. An employer wishes to determine how many of his employees are more than 60 years old. He has the age of each employee stored in a 1-dimensional array named *ages*. There are 100 employees.

   (a) State which standard algorithm could provide the basis for a program to produce this information?

1

   (b) Write the pseudocode for a program which will go through the array and count the number of employees whose age is over 60.

2

   (c) Implement the program using any high level language that you are familiar with.

2

(30)

[End of Section I]

SECTION II

Try to answer every question.

14. Digital images are often stored as bit-mapped graphics files.

   (a) State how bit-mapped images are stored.

1

   (b) State **two** techniques used to decrease the amount of storage required by bit-mapped graphics files.

2

   (c) State how many bytes would be required to store a 500 × 400 pixel image as:

   (i) An 8-bit grayscale bitmap

1

   (ii) A 16-bit colour bitmap

1

15. (a) Describe the **three** main functions of the control bus.

3

   (b) Describe **three** different methods of measuring the performance of a computer system.

3

   (c) State the meaning of the following terms as applied to printers:

   (i) Buffering

   (ii) Spooling

1, 1

   (d) Older printers are often connected to a computer via a Centronics or RS-232 interface, but these are no longer in common use. State two methods currently used to connect to printers?

2

16. (*a*) Describe the functions of the following networking devices, distinguishing clearly between them:

Marks

   (i) Hub   2

  (ii) Switch   2

 (iii) Router   2

(*b*) State the function of a Network Interface Card (NIC).   1

(*c*) State the **six** main functions of a single-user operating system.   6

(*d*) Describe **two** utility programs that you would expect to find on a computer system.   2

(*e*) Once a computer system is up and running it may still need maintenance. Describe **three** different types of maintenance that may be required.   3

17. Both compilers and interpreters are often used to translate high-level language programs into machine code during the software development process.

(*a*) Explain why it is useful to have two different translation tools available.   1

(*b*) State **two** advantages and **two** disadvantages of using a compiler rather than an interpreter.   4

18. A company has four different departments, each of which has a name and a department code as follows:

Department Name	Code
Manufacturing	10
Finance	11
Human Resources	12
Marketing	13

(*a*) Each employee has their Department Code stored in their personnel record. However, when printing pay slips the company wants the Department Name, rather than the Department Code to be printed.

  (i) Write a piece of pseudocode, showing how this task could be accomplished without using if-statements.   3

  (ii) Show how this could be implemented in a high-level language with which you are familiar.   3

(*b*) The Systems Manager has suggested that this task could be integrated into the Personnel system as a subprogram, but has left the programmer to choose whether to use a subroutine (procedure) or a function.

  (i) Explain the difference between a subroutine and a function.   2

  (ii) State what parameter passing mechanism should be used to pass the department code from the main program to the subprogram. Justify your answer.   2

(iii) The programmer has also considered the possibility of declaring the department code as a global variable, thereby avoiding the need to pass it as a parameter. Explain why this is not a good idea.

Marks

2

19. An oceanographer is researching the effects of climate change on water levels in the Firth of Clyde. She has obtained data regarding the minimum level recorded each year from 1900 to 1999. This data is stored in a 1-dimensional array of integers named *minlevels*. The data for 1900 is stored at position 1 in each array, the data for 1901 in position 2 and so on. She now wishes to analyse this data. She wants a program which will search through the array and find the lowest minimum level and the last year in which it occurred.

(a) Write the pseudocode for a program which will output this information.

6

(b) Implement your program using a high-level language with which you are familiar.

4

[End of Section II]

(60)

SECTION III

Select one sub-section of Section III.

Part A	Artificial Intelligence	Page 55	Questions 20 to 23
Part B	Computer Networking	Page 57	Questions 24 to 27
Part C	Multimedia Technology	Page 59	Questions 28 to 31

For the sub-section you have selected, try to answer every question.

Part A – Artificial Intelligence

20. Artificial intelligence is recognised as a rapidly changing field, with new developments taking place constantly.

(a) Describe the way in which the emphasis in artificial intelligence has changed in recent years.

2

(b) State two major differences between LISP and Prolog.

2

(c) Describe four practical problems which are still associated with AI, despite advances in hardware and software.

4

21. Mecanopetz has developed a mechanical dog, suitable for those whose lifestyle prevents them from having a normal pet. The dog demonstrates many features of AI, including computer vision, intelligent software and expert systems

(a) The dog uses an AI based computer vision system. Describe the **five** stages involved in computer vision.

5

(b) The dog's control systems are based on intelligent software. State **three** other examples of the use of intelligent software to control devices.

3

(c) The dog's behaviour is controlled by an expert system. Describe **five** disadvantages of expert systems.

5

22. (*a*) State **one** advantage and **one** disadvantage of each of the following types of   *Marks*
search:

    (i) breadth-first search   2

    (ii) depth-first search   2

(*b*)

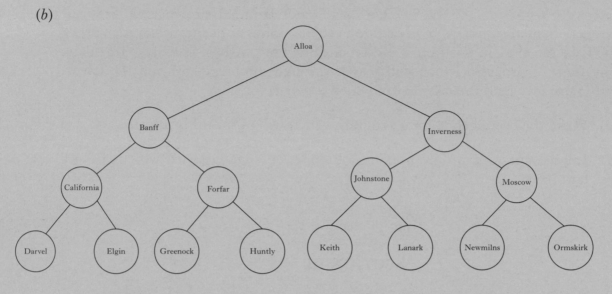

List the output that would be produced if the nodes in the above tree were
searched as follows:

    (i) breadth-first

    (ii) depth-first   3, 3

23. (*a*) You have been given the following information about a selection of stringed
instruments:

```
Violins, violas and cellos have four strings.
All four-stringed instruments are played with a bow.
Mandolins, mandolas and bouzoukis have 8 strings.
All eight-stringed instruments are played with a plectrum.
Banjos have 5 strings.
Banjos are played with a plectrum
Guitars have six strings
Guitars are played with a plectrum
```

Construct a semantic net to illustrate the relationships between these
instruments and their characteristics.   8

(*b*) The following Prolog knowledge base represent the characteristics of a range
of musical instruments and can be used to identify specific instruments or
groups of instruments:

```
1.  neck(violin, short).
2.  neck(mandolin, short).
3.  neck(ukelele, short).
4.  neck(viola, medium).
5.  neck(mandola, medium).
6.  neck(tenor_banjo, medium).
7.  neck(bouzouki, long).
8.  neck(g_banjo, long).
9.  neck(cello, long).
10. neck(guitar, long).
```

```
11. strings(violin, 4).
12. strings(mandolin, 8).
13. strings(ukelele, 4).
14. strings(viola, 4).
15. strings(mandola, 8).
16. strings(tenor_banjo, 4).
17. strings(cello, 4).
18. strings(guitar, 6).
19. strings(bouzouki, 8).
20. strings(g_banjo, 5).

21. playedwith(violin, bow).
22. playedwith(mandolin, plectrum).
23. playedwith(ukelele, plectrum).
24. playedwith(viola, bow).
25. playedwith(mandola, plectrum).
26. playedwith(tenor_banjo, plectrum).
27. playedwith(cello, bow).
28. playedwith(guitar, plectrum).
29. playedwith(bouzouki, plectrum).
30. playedwith(g_banjo, plectrum).

31. instrument(A, X, Y, Z) :- neck(A,X), strings(A,Y),
    playedwith(A,Z).
```

    (i) What output will the following query produce:

```
instrument(A,_,8,_).
```
2

   (ii) Trace the execution of the following query:

```
instrument(A,long,5,plectrum).
```

Your answer should make correct use of the terms 'subgoal' and 'instantiate'.   9

[End of Section III – Part A]

SECTION III

Part B – Computer Networking

Try to answer every question.

24. (*a*) Describe the **four** classes of IP addresses, indicating what each class is used for and the way in which the available bits are allocated between the network address and the host addresses.   8

    (*b*) State which layer of the OSI Network Model is responsible for each of the following tasks:

      (i) Routing packets between networks

     (ii) Breaking files up into packets and reassembling them at the destination

    (iii) Data format conversion, encryption and compression

    (iv) Cabling types and signal levels

    (v) Size and addressing of packets, error checking and correction

	Marks

(vi) Initiating, managing and terminating communications between computers.

(vii) Communication between application programs and the network.   7

25. (*a*) Microbrowsers are used to display normal web pages on handheld devices. Describe **two** techniques they use to accomplish this.   2

(*b*) Documents designed for display on mobile devices are normally written in WML rather than HTML. Describe **two** ways in which an WML document differs from an XML document.   4

(*c*) State **two** advantages of e-commerce for each of the following:

   (i) Retailers   2

   (ii) Customers   2

(*d*) State **two** advantages and **two** disadvantages of teleworking.   4

(*e*) Describe the implications of the Regulation of Investigatory Powers Act for personal privacy on the internet?   3

26. (*a*) State the **three** main requirements for network security.   3

(*b*) Explain the difference between active and passive attacks in a computer network.   2

(*c*) Describe **three** different techniques that can be used by a firewall to prevent intruders from gaining access to a computer network.   3

(*d*) State **two** disadvantages of using content-filtering software to control network access.   2

(*e*) State the meaning of the term "walled garden".   1

27. (*a*) Explain the difference between synchronous transmission and asynchronous transmission.   2

(*b*) Explain how packet switching differs from circuit switching.   2

(*c*) Describe the operation of the CSMA/CD network protocol.   3

    (50)

[End of Section III – Part B]

SECTION III

Marks

Part C – Multimedia Technology

Try to Answer every question.

28. Bit-mapped graphics are frequently used to store photographs and other images. Several different file formats and compression techniques are currently used.

   (*a*) Describe **two** different bit-mapped graphics file formats.   2

   (*b*) Describe **two** different compression techniques.   2

   (*c*) Describe the use of RGB colour codes to represent colours in a computer system.   2

   (*d*) State one advantage and one disadvantage of resampling an image at a higher resoultion.   2

29. Mobile Music Videos is a company which specialises in recording live music performances and converting them to a format suitable for display on handheld devices.

   (*a*) Describe the role of the array CCD in a video camera in capturing video.   2

   (*b*) Describe how video data can be stored in

   (i) Uncompressed format   2

   (ii) Compressed format   2

   (*c*) Calculate the amount of storage required for a 30 minute video measuring 320 × 240, recorded at 30 fps in 24-bit colour. (Show all working.)   2

   (*d*) Describe a technique used to include sound in digital video files.   2

30. McTavish Marketing produces product marketing videos using a combination of animated vector graphics and synthesised music files.

   (*a*) State **two** advantages and **two** disadvantages of storing music as MIDI data.   4

   (*b*) State **five** characteristics of music stored as MIDI data.   5

   (*c*) State **four** advantages of storing graphics in vector image format.   4

   (*d*) Describe the storage of vector graphics images as SVG files.   2

31. Circo de Luna is an international circus company, famous for their visually-spectacular performances and the accompanying music. To date they have relied mainly on live performances to earn income, but they have now decided to set up a new division to market multimedia products via a web site.

Marks

(*a*) Describe the three types of software they will need to obtain in order to create:

   (i) Web pages   2

   (ii) Multimedia applications   2

   (iii) Presentations   2

(*b*) The company has an enormous archive of high-quality video footage of their performances, recorded over a period of several years. Unfortunately the sound quality is poor, so they have decided to record new soundtracks. Calculate how much storage will be required for an hour-long stereo soundtrack, sampled at 44.1 kHz with a sampling depth of 16 bits? (Show all the working for your calculations.)   2

(*c*) The company has decided to purchase a high-quality sound card in order to make the necessary recordings. Describe in detail the function of each of the following components of a sound card:

   (i) ADC   3

   (ii) DSP   3

   (iii) DAC   3

(50)

[End of Section III – Part C]

Worked Answers

SECTION I

1.   *(a)*

> This question is about the binary representation of positive integers. The number of positive integers that can be represented by X binary digits is 2^X (2 to the power x). However, remember that the range always starts at 0, so the range that can be represented will always be 0 to $2^X - 1$.

16 bits are required to represent numbers in the range 0 to 65535. (1 mark)

(b)

> **HINT**
>
> You must know about the binary representation of floating-point numbers to answer this question correctly. These numbers are represented by **M × 2^E**, where the **mantissa (M)** is a binary fraction starting with a 1 and the **exponent (E)** is a binary integer. The mantissa determines the degree of accuracy or precision with which numbers can be represented, while the exponent determines the range of numbers that can be represented. So, increasing the number of bits assigned to the mantissa will increase the accuracy with which the number can be represented, at the expense of decreasing the range of numbers that can be represented.

Increasing the number of bits assigned to the mantissa of a floating point number will increase the accuracy or precision of the number. (1 mark)

TOP EXAM TIP

You should know the formula for calculating the range of integers that can be represented by a given number of bits. Don't forget to subtract 1. You should also know the ranges that can be represented by the most common numbers of bits,

4 bits: 0 to 15   8 bits: 0 to 255   16 bits: 0 to 65,535   32 bits: 0 to 4,294,967,295

2.

> This is a question about *vector graphics*, a method of storing images as a list of objects (eg: lines, circles etc.), each with its own attributes. This is often contrasted with *bit-mapped graphics* which store images as a series of codes representing individual pixels.

Vector graphics (1 mark) stores images as a list of objects, each with its own attributes.

3.

> This question is about *processor busses*, groups of wires which connect the CPU with the main memory.

The data bus is used to transfer data between the CPU and the main memory. (1 mark)

> **HINT**
>
> There are three *busses*, the *data bus*, the *control lines* and the *address bus*. The data bus is used to transfer data between the CPU and the memory, the *address bus* to specify the memory address being used and the *control lines* to carry control signals, such as starting a read or write operation.

4.

This question is about the *fetch-execute cycle*, which consists of fetching an instruction from main memory (1 mark) and executing it in the CPU (1 mark).

The fetch-execute cycle consists of fetching an instruction from main memory (1 mark) and executing it in the CPU (1 mark).

HINT

The fetch-execute cycle is normally regarded as a five-stage process, ie:

FETCH:

- The address of the next instruction to be executed is placed on the address bus
- The read line is activated
- The data stored in the specified memory location is transferred via the data bus to a CPU register

EXECUTE:

- The instruction is decoded by the CPU
- The instruction is executed by the CPU

However, only two marks are available for this question, so just a brief description is required.

5.

This question is about current trends in the development of backing storage devices.

Hard disks are becoming faster (1 mark) and storage capacities are increasing (1 mark).

HINT

There are a number of current trends in this area of which you should be aware, eg:

Hard Disks:

- Devices are becoming faster. 5400 rpm disks have largely been replaced by 7200 rpm disks
- Capacities are becoming larger: storage capacities in excess of 1TB are now commonplace.
- Disk cache memories are becoming larger.
- Serial interfaces (SATA) are replacing parallel (ATA) interfaces.
- Disks are becoming cheaper.

Flash Memory:

- Storage capacities are increasing
- Transfer rates are improving
- Devices are becoming smaller (eg: micro SD)
- Devices are getting cheaper

Only two trends need to be mentioned in your answer.

6. (*a*)

This question is about the components of a computer network.

A node (1 mark) is any device attached to a computer network. A channel is a connection or pathway between nodes (1 mark).

HINT

A node is any device attached to a network, eg: a server, a workstation or a printer. A channel is a path between nodes, eg: copper or fibre-optic cable or a wireless connection.

(b)

This question requires you to be familiar with the switching devices used to link the different nodes of a computer network.

A switch gives each node access to the full bandwidth available on the network. (1 mark)

Switches make a direct connection between each of the nodes on a network. (1 mark)

HINT

When a hub receives a message from a node it broadcasts it to all the other nodes on the network, often after amplifying it. Hubs share the available bandwidth between all the nodes on the network. They are available in various sizes for both home and professional networks. Switches make direct connections between different nodes, so that when a message is received rom one node it can be forwarded directly to the specified destination, rather than being broadcast to the entire network. A switch gives each node access to the full bandwidth available on the network.

TOP EXAM TIP

It is important to be thoroughly familiar with the functions of hubs, switches and routers and the differences between them.

Hubs connect all the nodes on a network. When they receive a signal from one node they amplify it before broadcasting it to all the other nodes on the network. Stackable hubs with up to 24 ports can be connected together to form large LANs. Hubs share the available bandwidth between all the nodes connected to a network.

Switches also connect nodes to a network, but each connected node has access to the full bandwidth of the network. A switch makes point-to-point connections between nodes, so there is no need to broadcast messages – they can be transmitted directly to the destination node. Network performance does not deteriorate as additional nodes are added.

Routers receive packets and forward them over the most efficient route to a destination. They can analyse networks to determine the optimum route. They have their own processor and can store information about the paths between nodes. Routers are used to partition large networks into smaller subnetworks, combine small networks into larger internetworks, connect LANs to telecommunications systems and route traffic across the Internet.

7.   (a)

This question covers the different types of computer virus.

A macro virus attaches itself to word processor document, rather than executable files. (1 mark)

HINT

There are a number of computer viruses, including *file virus, boot sector virus, macro virus* and *program virus*. The type of virus which attaches itself to word processor files is known as a macro virus.

(b)

This question is about the various actions which can be carried out by a virus, namely replication, camouflage, watching and delivery.

Replication is the process by which a virus copies itself. This can happen many times before the virus is activated.

Camouflage is a method where a virus changes its signature by inserting dummy lines of code within its own code to stop it being recognised by anti-virus software.

Watching is the process by which a virus waits for a particular date to be reached or event to occur before activating itself.

The process by which a virus creates additional copies of itself is known as replication. (1 mark)

(c)

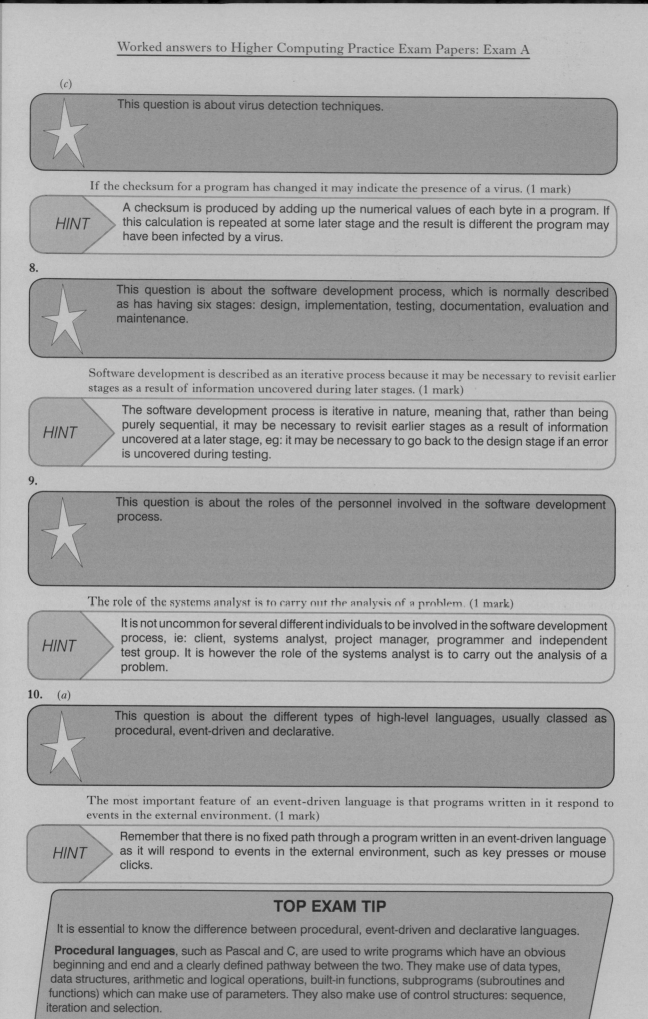

This question is about virus detection techniques.

If the checksum for a program has changed it may indicate the presence of a virus. (1 mark)

HINT
A checksum is produced by adding up the numerical values of each byte in a program. If this calculation is repeated at some later stage and the result is different the program may have been infected by a virus.

8.

This question is about the software development process, which is normally described as has having six stages: design, implementation, testing, documentation, evaluation and maintenance.

Software development is described as an iterative process because it may be necessary to revisit earlier stages as a result of information uncovered during later stages. (1 mark)

HINT
The software development process is iterative in nature, meaning that, rather than being purely sequential, it may be necessary to revisit earlier stages as a result of information uncovered at a later stage, eg: it may be necessary to go back to the design stage if an error is uncovered during testing.

9.

This question is about the roles of the personnel involved in the software development process.

The role of the systems analyst is to carry out the analysis of a problem. (1 mark)

HINT
It is not uncommon for several different individuals to be involved in the software development process, ie: client, systems analyst, project manager, programmer and independent test group. It is however the role of the systems analyst is to carry out the analysis of a problem.

10.   (a)

This question is about the different types of high-level languages, usually classed as procedural, event-driven and declarative.

The most important feature of an event-driven language is that programs written in it respond to events in the external environment. (1 mark)

HINT
Remember that there is no fixed path through a program written in an event-driven language as it will respond to events in the external environment, such as key presses or mouse clicks.

TOP EXAM TIP

It is essential to know the difference between procedural, event-driven and declarative languages.

Procedural languages, such as Pascal and C, are used to write programs which have an obvious beginning and end and a clearly defined pathway between the two. They make use of data types, data structures, arithmetic and logical operations, built-in functions, subprograms (subroutines and functions) which can make use of parameters. They also make use of control structures: sequence, iteration and selection.

Event-driven languages, such as Visual Basic, produce programs which respond to external events, such as a key press or a mouse click. Instructions are not executed in a defined sequence but depend on the order in which events happen. They can look very similar to programs written in a procedural language but the way that they are executed is completely different.

(b)

This question is about string operations.

The two main string operations are (i) substring, which allows characters in specified positions to be extracted from a string (1 mark) and (ii) concatenation, which allows strings to be joined together. (1 mark)

HINT

There are two main string operations: substring, which allows characters in specified positions to be extracted from a string, usually from the left, middle or right, and concatenation, which allows strings to be joined together.

(c)

This question is about translation programs, ie: compilers and interpreters.

The main advantage of using compiled programs is that they run faster than interpreted programs. (1 mark)

HINT

A compiler translates a whole program into executable form prior to execution, whereas an interpreter translates and executes a program line by line. Compiled programs run faster as translation only needs to take place once, rather than being required every time the program is executed. Interpreted programs run more slowly as each line requires to be translated before it is executed. However, interpreters can be useful during the software development process as the programmer does not need to wait for the whole program to be translated before running it.

11. (a)

This question is about the different types of variables used in computer programs, the main ones being integer (used to store whole numbers) real or floating-point, used to store numbers which have a fractional part, string, used to store character strings, boolean, used to store variables which can only have two values and one-dimensional array, used to store groups of variables of the same type.

Boolean variables are used to store data items which can only have two values, TRUE or FALSE. (1 mark)

HINT

Boolean variables are used to store data items which can only have two values, TRUE or FALSE, eg: ON/OFF, YES/NO. They are often represented internally by a single binary digit (bit) which can take the values 0 or 1.

(b) A real variable would be best suited to storing a weight. (1 mark)

HINT

The weight of an item is unlikely to be a whole number, it will probably have a fractional part, eg: 1.65 kg, 2.2 lbs etc. The best choice to store it is therefore a real variable.

(c) Local variables exist only within a given subprogram and their value is generally lost on exiting the subprogram. (1 mark) Global variables are accessible throughout the whole program and generally keep their value throughout the entire duration of the program. (1 mark)

HINT

This question is about the scope of variables. Local variables exist only within a given subprogram and their value is generally lost on exiting the subprogram. Global variables are accessible throughout the whole program and generally keep their value throughout the entire duration of the program.

TOP EXAM TIP

One useful way of knowing when to use real or integer variables it to remember that real variables are used for **measured** data, eg: weights, heights, distances etc. whereas integer variables are used for **counted** data, number of students in a class, number of vehicles in a car park, etc.

12.

This question is about algorithms. An algorithm is an explicit, step-by-step procedure for solving a problem.

(a) Standard algorithms are those which occur frequently in computer programs (1 mark), such as finding the minimum or maximum value in a list. (1 mark)

(b) Three common algorithms which often occur in computer programs are:

- Linear search (1 mark)

- Counting occurrences (1 mark)

- Finding minimum or maximum (1 mark)

HINT

There are four standard algorithms which occur frequently in computer programs: linear search, counting occurrences, finding maximum value and finding minimum value. The last two are effectively variations of the same algorithm. A further variation involves finding the location of the minimum or maximum value.

TOP EXAM TIP

The standard algorithms always appear in the Higher Computing exam, so you should know them inside out. You should be able to express them both in pseudocode and in a high-level language. You will generally be required to apply a standard algorithm to the solution of a problem, rather than simply give a statement of the algorithm.

SECTION II

13.

(a) Flash memory cards are small and lightweight (1 mark) and have fast access speeds. (1 mark)

(b) A bit-mapped image is stored as a two-dimensional grid of binary integers, each of which represents a single pixel. (1 mark)

(c) 16,777,216 different colours can be represented. (1 mark)

HINT

This question is about the bit-depth of bit-mapped graphics, ie: the number of bits used to represent each pixel. The number of colours the can be represented by an X-bit integer is 2^X, so for a 24-bit integer this would be $2^{24} = 16,777,216$. 24-bit colour is sometimes referred to as "True Colour" and corresponds roughly to the number of discrete colours that can be viewed by the human eye.

(d) The storage required is

    $2048 \times 1535 \times 24$ bits
= 75448320 bits (1 mark)
= 75448320/8 = 9431040 bytes
= 9431040/1024 = 9210 kilobytes
= 9210/1024 = 8.99 megabytes (1 mark)

HINT

This question is about the storage space required for bit-mapped graphics. This can be calculated from the formula:

width (in pixels) × height (in pixels) X bit-depth

which will give the amount of storage required in bits.

TOP EXAM TIP

Make sure you know how to calculate the storage requirements for a bit-mapped image as this type of question frequently crops up. You may be given the size of the image in inches rather than pixels, in which case you would need to start the calculation by converting each measurement to pixels by multiplying the number of inches by the number of dots per inch (DPI). For example, if the image was said to be 9" by 4" at 200 DPI then the number of pixels would be 1800 × 800. Always show all your working for calculations.

14. (*a*) (i) Registers are small storage areas within the CPU used for storing temporary values, for example when carrying out calculations. (1 mark)

   (ii) Cache is fast memory that sits between the CPU and the main memory. It is used to speed up transfers between the CPU and the main memory. (1 mark)

   (iii) The main memory consists of RAM chips. It is used to store the programs currently being executed and the data they are processing. (1 mark)

   (iv) Backing storage consists of hard disks and/or solid state memory devices. It is used to store programs and data which can be loaded into main memory. (1 mark)

   (*b*) Increasing the cache memory will improve performance. (1 mark)

   (*c*) A 32-bit address bus can address 4 Gigabytes of memory. (1 mark)

> *HINT*
>
> This question is about the address bus, which is used to specify a physical location in memory. When a processor wants to read or write to a memory location, it places the location on the address bus. The value to be read or written is sent on the data bus. The width of the address bus determines the amount of memory a system can address, eg: a 32-bit address bus can address 232 (4,294,967,296) bytes, or 4GB, of memory.

TOP EXAM TIP

This topic crops up frequently in the Higher Computing examination. It is important that you can describe following elements of computer memory: registers, cache, main memory and backing storage and distinguish between them in terms of function and speed of access.

15.

This question is about peer-to-peer and client-server networks.

   (*a*) any two of the following points would be worth a mark each.

   On a client-server network there are two different types of machines, clients and servers. On a peer-to-peer network all machines are equal and function as both client and server. (1 mark)

   Client server networks offer better security as they can be controlled from a central location. (1 mark)

   It is easier to back up data on a client server network, since it is stored on a central server. In peer-to-peer networks each machine must be backed up individually. (1 mark)

   In a client-server network software can be installed on a central server and distributed to other machines from there. On a peer-to-per network software needs to be installed on each individual machine. (1 mark)

   Peer-to-peer networks only function efficiently with small numbers of machines. Client server networks can have very large numbers of machines. (1 mark)

> *HINT*
>
> A client-server network has two different types of machines: clients and servers. There may be several different types of server, eg: file server, print server, media serve etc. Security is good, as logon access can be controlled by a central server. All data is stored on a server, making it easy to back-up and restore. Software only needs to be installed on the server and can be distributed to other machines from there. Client server networks can operate efficiently with large numbers of machines, often running into hundreds, or even thousands.
>
> A peer-to-peer network has no central servers – all the machines are equal. Security is weak as there is no central control. Data is stored on individual machines, meaning that each machine requires its own backups. Software must also be installed on each individual machine. Peer-to-peer networks can become very inefficient if there are any more than eight or so machines involved.

   (*b*) any two of the following points would be worth a mark each.

   Wireless networks allow network access in locations which would be difficult or inconvenient to cable. (1 mark)

   Wireless networks allow mobile users to log on from laptops or PDAs at any location which offers wireless access. (1 mark)

   The security of wireless networks has improved significantly. (1 mark)

   The speed of wireless networks has improved with each generation. (1 mark)

(c)   Network operating systems have improved. (1 mark)

Browsers have improved. (1 mark)

Data transmission media (and hence speeds) have improved. (1 mark)

Client and server hardware has improved in terms of processor speeds, memory size and hard disk capacity. (1 mark)

(d)

HINT — This question is about the legal aspects of using computer networks. In this case, the laws which are likely to be involved are the Computer Misuse Act, which prohibits the unauthorised use of a computer and the Copyright, Design and Patents Act, which prohibits the theft of intellectual property, including music and literature.

The two laws which the students are likely to have broken are the Computer Misuse Act (1 mark) and the Copyright, Designs and Patents Act. (1 mark)

TOP EXAM TIP

You should be familiar with the names and some brief details of the principal laws which regulate the use of computer networks. The most important ones are the Computer Misuse Act, the Copyright, Designs and Patents Act and the Data Protection Act.

16.

This question is about the type of applications packages used to produce multimedia applications.

(a)   An authoring package. (1 mark)

HINT — The most general type of package that can be used is an authoring package, which should be able to handle all or most of the required tasks.

(b)   Any three of the following would be acceptable:

Scripting (1 mark)
Audio capture/editing/manipulation (1 mark)
Video capture/editing/manipulation (1 mark)
Text entry/editing (1 mark)
Bit-mapped graphics capture/manipulation (1 mark)
Vector graphics creation/manipulation (1 mark)

(c)   Audio editing (1 mark) and bit-mapped graphics editing. (1 mark)

HINT — Authoring packages of this nature would routinely include some kind of scripting facility to tie the whole thing together and the ability to edit/manipulate the source media, eg: audio, video, text and image files.

Although many authoring packages can handle all of these, they seldom reach the standard of the best-of-breed standalone applications, so a company with very specific needs in a defined area, eg: audio or video editing, may need to supplement the authoring package with specialist software for these areas.

(d)

This question is about bit-mapped graphics file formats.

They should be stored in JPEG (.jpg) format. (1 mark)

HINT — TIFF files would be the highest quality, but they are very large. GIF files are good for storing cartoons, technical photographs and so on, but not so good for photographs. JPEG files are good for photographs, but there will be some loss due to compression.

(e)   Model 1 is a better choice due to its larger main memory (1 mark), faster CPU/faster hard drive (1 mark), higher resolution screen (1 mark) and lower cost. (1 mark)

HINT

This question is about selecting suitable hardware for a particular task. Model 1 Has more main memory (4GB) which should make it significantly faster, a faster CPU speed and a faster hard disk (a significant advantage). Model 1's 21 inch monitor will be capable of operating at a higher resolution (1600 × 1200) than Model 2's 19 inch monitor (1280 × 1024). Model 2 has a larger cache memory, which will improve its speed, but this is of little importance compared with CPU speed, disk speed and amount of main memory. Model 2 has a quad core CPU, but there is little software that can take advantage of this. It also has a larger hard drive, but 600 GB is large enough for most practical purposes.

(f) Any two of the following, for one mark each:

buffering (1 mark)
data format conversion (1 mark)
voltage conversion (1 mark)
protocol conversion (1 mark)
handling of status signals (1 mark)

HINT

This question is about the functions of an interface. The main functions are as follows:

- Buffering: storing data temporarily to compensate for differences in speed of devices
- Data format conversion: eg: analogue to digital or serial to parallel
- Voltage conversion: peripherals generally work on higher voltages than the CPU
- Protocol conversion: speed of transmission and size / structure of data packets
- Handling of status signals: eg: signaling that a peripheral is ready to accept data

17.

This question is about the characteristics of procedural languages.

(a) Programs written in a procedural language have a specific start and end-point (1 mark) and a clearly defined route through the program. (1 mark)

HINT

Programs written in a procedural language have a specific start and end-point and a clearly defined route through the program. Other features of procedural languages include data types (real, integer, boolean, string), data structures (array), arithmetic and logical operations, built-in functions, subprograms (functions and procedures) which can transfer data by means of parameters and control constructs (sequence, iteration (repetition) and selection.

(b) Scripting languages allow users to write programs or scripts to customise an applications package (1 mark) or to automate repetitive tasks. (1 mark)

HINT

This question is about the benefits of scripting languages. These are supplied with applications packages and allow users to write programs or scripts to customise the package or automate repetitive tasks. They can be used to write macros, ie: sequences of actions stored as scripting language instructions.

(c) Record the steps involved in setting up the required headers and footers (1 mark) and store these as a macro. (1 mark)

HINT This question is about the use of macros to extend or customise an applications package.

(d)
```
Select Case Day
Case 1
    Print "Monday"
Case 2
    Print "Tuesday"
Case 3
    Print "Wednesday"
Case 4
    Print "Thursday"
Case 5
    Print "Friday"
Case 6
    Print "Saturday"
Case 7
    Print "Sunday"
End Select
```

TOP EXAM TIP

It is important to be familiar with the use of the Case statement. The same problem could be solved by using nested If statements, but the solution is less elegant.

HINT > This question is about the use of the Case statement (or similar) to handle selection from multiple alternatives.

(e)
```
Sub CalcAvg(By Value Num1 As Integer,
            By Value Num2 As Integer,
            By Value Num3 As Integer,
            By Ref Avg As Real)
    Let Avg = (Num1 + Num2 + Num3)/3
End Sub
```

Marks will be allocated for structure of subroutine (1 mark), parameter types (1 mark), parameter-passing mechanism (1 mark), calculation (1 mark).

(f) When using a value parameter the value of a variable is copied and passed to the subroutine. Any changes made to the value within the subroutine will not be passed back to the main program. (1 mark) When using a reference parameter, the storage location of a variable is passed to the subroutine. If any changes to the value are made in the subroutine, the value will also change in the main program. (1 mark)

TOP EXAM TIP

You should ensure that you are thoroughly familiar with all aspects of parameters and parameter passing mechanisms. You should be aware that Call by Value is used when no data is to be returned from the subprogram and Call by Reference when a value needs to be returned.

18. (a)
```
Let Forename = "Duncan"
Let Surname = "Macdonald"                              (1 mark)
Let Headuser = First(Forename, 1)                      (1 mark)
Let Tailuser = First(Surname, 5)                       (1 mark)
Let Username = Headuser & Tailuser                     (1 mark)
Print Username
```

(b)
```
program createuser (input, output);
uses crt;
var
forename, surname, username, headuser, tailuser: string;
begin
    forename := 'Duncan';
    surname := 'Macdonald';

    headuser := Copy(forename,1,1);
    tailuser := Copy(surname,1,5);                     (1 mark)

    username := Concat(headuser, tailuser);            (1 mark)

    writeln(username)
end.
```

(c)
```
Let Location = 0
Let I = 0
Read (Searchname)
Do
    Add 1 to I
    If Namearray(I) = Searchname
        Let Location = I
Loop Until Namearray(I) = NULL                         (1 mark)
If Location is not equal to 0
    Print Username " found at position " Location       (1 mark)
Else
    Print Username " not found"                         (1 mark)
```

(d)
```
Let Found = FALSE
Let Location = 0
Let I = 0
Read (Searchname)
Do
    Add 1 to I
    If Namearray(I) = Searchname
        Let Location = I
        Let Found = TRUE                                (1 mark)
Loop Until Found or (Namearray(I) = NULL)              (1 mark)
If Location is not equal to 0
    Print Username " found at position " Location
Else

    Print Username " not found"
```

> *HINT* This question is about modifying the standard algorithm to stop when a match has been found. This is accomplished by setting a boolean variable to TRUE when a match is found and testing the boolean variable on each iteration of the loop.

TOP EXAM TIP

You should be familiar with all the standard algorithms (counting the items in a list, searching a list, finding minimum or maximum) and their variations. You should also be able to apply the algorithms to specified situations, rather than simply quoting them.

SECTION III

Part A – Artificial Intelligence

19.

 This question is about various aspects of Artificial Intelligence, including the changes that have taken place over the years and the hardware developments that have affected these.

(a) It is difficult to produce an accurate and agreed definition of intelligence because there are so many different factors involved, (1 mark) including language, learning, cognitive ability, problem-solving, memory and creativity. (1 mark)

(b) Early AI projects tried to model the activity of the human brain. (1 mark) Current projects concentrate more on producing systems which exhibit intelligent behaviour. (1 mark)

(c) Faster processors mean that computers can carry out calculations and perform searches more quickly, allowing problems that would once have taken impossibly long to be solved in a reasonable time. (1 mark) Cheaper and faster memory allows more data to be store in RAM, meaning that more complex problems can be tackled. (1 mark)

20.

 This question is about two major areas of research in artificial intelligence, Neural Networks and Natural Language Processing (NLP).

(a) The four major components or a neural network are artificial neurons, (1 mark) the links connecting them, (1 mark) the weight or threshold value given to each artificial neuron (1 mark) and the layers (inner, hidden and output) which generate signals. (1 mark)

(b) Neural networks are much smaller than the human brain, (1 mark) which is thought to contain up to 10 billion neurons. They can also operate much more rapidly than the human brain. (1 mark)

TOP EXAM TIP

Make sure that you are thoroughly familiar with the four components of neural networks: artificial neurons, links, weights and layers.

(c) Aspects of human language that can be the source of difficulties in Natural Language Processing include the following:

- Ambiguity as to the meaning of words, eg: "lead" could be a type of metal or the graphite in a pencil. (1 mark)
- Words which sound the same can have completely different meanings, eg: "two", "too", "to". (1 mark)
- Grammar is inconsistent, eg: the plural of "foot" is "feet", but the plural of "boot" is "boots". (1 mark)
- The meaning of words can change, eg: "text" used to be a noun describing printed words, now it can also be a verb meaning to send an SMS message. (1 mark)

(d) Areas where Natural Language Processing techniques can usefully be applied include Machine Translation (1 mark) and Speech Recognition. (1 mark)

21.

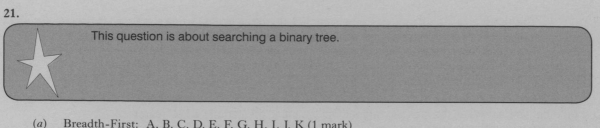

This question is about searching a binary tree.

(a)   Breadth-First: A, B, C, D, E, F, G, H, I, J, K (1 mark)

Depth-First: A, B, D, H, I, E, J, C, F, G, K (1 mark)

(b)   To carry out a breadth-first search the entire tree must be stored in memory as there is no way of knowing in advance which node will be processed next. (1 mark)

(c)   In the depth-first search a branch can be removed from memory if it has been followed to the end without finding a match for the target.   (1 mark)

(d)   Heuristics can be used to reduce the amount of time and/or space required for a search by eliminating the least likely solutions. (1 mark)

22.

This question is about declarative languages.

(a)   The software development process is every bit as applicable to declarative language programming as to any other type of programming. (1 mark) Analysis is still required to find out what the program is expected to do. (1 mark) The Design stage will involve determining the structure of the knowledge base and the rules to be applied. (1 mark) Implementation will involve coding the knowledge base and rules in a declarative language. (1 mark) Testing will be required to ensure that the program functions correctly. (1 mark) Documentation, including User and Technical guides, will still be required. (1 mark) Maintenance can be required in declarative programs, due to changes in the knowledge base or the rule to be applied. (1 mark)

(1 mark for each valid point made, up to a maximum of five.)

(b)   (i)   Recursion

The following code shows a recursive definition of ancestor:

```
parent(iain,murdo). /* murdo is iain's parent   */
parent(murdo,duncan). /* duncan is murdo's parent */
parent(duncan,morag). /* morag is duncan's parent */          (1 mark)
ancestor(X,Y) :- parent(X,Y).

/* If Y is a parent of X, then Y is an ancestor of X */

ancestor(X,Y) :- parent(X,Z),

                      ancestor(Z,Y).
/* if Y is an ancestor of Z and Z is a parent of X,
then Y is an ancestor of X */                                  (1 mark)
```

Queries can now be run using this function, eg:

```
| ?- ancestor(iain,duncan).
yes

| ?- ancestor(duncan,iain).
No                                                             (1 mark)
```

(ii)   Negation

It's possible to reduce the number of rules in a Prolog program if a rule can be stated as a negation of a fact, eg:

```
female(morag).
male(X) :- not female(X).                                      (1 mark)
```

If we now submit the query male(morag) we get the expected result:

```
| ?- male(morag).
```

No   (1 mark)

However, if we submit the query male(shona) the result seems a bit odd:

```
| ?- male(shona).
yes
```

This is because the Prolog interpreter assumes that the database is a closed world. If it cannot prove something is true, it assumes that it is false. This is also known as negation as failure, ie: something is false if Prolog cannot prove it true, given the facts and rules in its database. (1 mark)

(iii)   Inheritance

We need some kind of rule that allows us to state that if X is a member of a particular group then X should inherit all the properties of that group. (1 mark) This can be accomplished by the following recursive rule:

```
has(X,Y) :- is_a(X,G), has(G,Y) (1 mark)
```

This means X has Y if X is in group G and G has Y. For example, Fido has a tail if Fido is a dog and dogs have tails. (1 mark)

TOP EXAM TIP

Make sure that you are familiar with the features of Prolog or another declarative language, eg: multi-argument clauses, complex queries, negation, inheritance and especially, recursive and non-recursive rules.)

23.

This question is about the use of knowledge bases in declarative language programming.

(a)   X = teith.   (1 mark)

HINT   Take care! The omission of the capitalized variable X would lose a mark.

(b)   First sub-goal tributary(Y,X) is matched at line 1 (1 mark)
      Y is instantiated to clyde and X is instantiated to white_cart (1 mark)
      Second sub-goal destination (north_sea, clyde) fails to make a match (1 mark)
      Backtrack to line 2 and continue search (1 mark)
      First sub-goal tributary(Y,X)) is matched at line 2 (1 mark)
      Y is instantiated to forth and X to teith (1 mark)
      Second sub-goal destination (north_sea, forth) is matched at line 11 (1 mark)
      Both subgoals have succeeded, so the goal has succeeded (1 mark)
      The first result of the query is teith (1 mark)

(c)   Facts and rules which are more likely to provide a solution should be paced close to the beginning of the program (1 mark) as this will reduce the time needed to find a solution. (1 mark)

TOP EXAM TIP

Make sure that you can carry out a manual trace of the pathway through a Prolog program as this nearly always appears in the exam. You should be able to highlight examples of sub-goals, backtracking and instantiation.

SECTION III
Part B – Computer Networking

24.

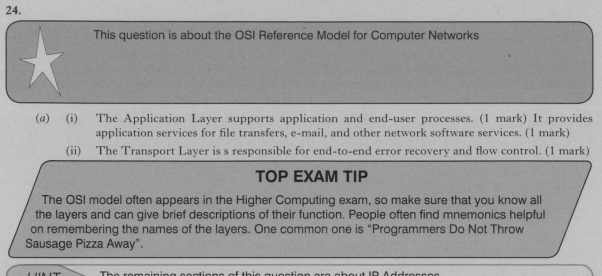

This question is about the OSI Reference Model for Computer Networks

(a) (i) The Application Layer supports application and end-user processes. (1 mark) It provides application services for file transfers, e-mail, and other network software services. (1 mark)

(ii) The Transport Layer is s responsible for end-to-end error recovery and flow control. (1 mark)

TOP EXAM TIP

The OSI model often appears in the Higher Computing exam, so make sure that you know all the layers and can give brief descriptions of their function. People often find mnemonics helpful on remembering the names of the layers. One common one is "Programmers Do Not Throw Sausage Pizza Away".

HINT > The remaining sections of this question are about IP Addresses.

(b) (i) An IP address is a 32-bit binary integer, but it is more often written as a group of four octets, usually written as decimal integers in the range 0–255, separated by dots, eg: 192.168.0.1 (1 mark)

(ii) IP addresses are divided into classes to allow a larger number of hosts to be addressed (1 mark) by splitting the address into a network ID and a host ID. (1 mark)

(iii) A Class C IP address uses the first three octets for the Network Id (1 mark) and the remaining octets for the Host Id. (1 mark)

(iv) A URL is converted to an IP address by requesting a Domain Name Server to look up the URL in a table and supply the corresponding IP address. (1 mark) The process is known as name resolution. (1 mark)

TOP EXAM TIP

Make sure that you are familiar with the use of Domain Name Servers to convert URLs to IP addresses.

(c) (i) The TELNET protocol is used for logging on to remote servers, (1 mark) for example, web servers. (1 mark)

(ii) The SMTP protocol is used for transmitting outgoing emails (1 mark) from a mail server to the destination address. (1 mark)

25.

This question is about the increasing use of wireless networks.

(a) Wireless Application Protocol (WAP). (1 mark)

(b) Limited screen area means they can often only display part of a page (1 mark). They can't deal with all types of data, eg: some have problems with Flash, streaming video etc. (1 mark) Reformatting of pages for small screens doesn't always work well. (1 mark)

(1 mark for each valid point up to a maximum of 2 marks.)

(c) A WML-page is known as a "deck". Every deck contains one or more cards. A regular page is a card and the home page is the deck. The suffix for WML-cards is .wml. The basic layout of a WML page is as follows:

```
<wml>
  <card id="Card1" title="First Card ">
    <p>
      <!- WML example -->
      This is a simple WML Card.
    </p>
  </card>
</wml>
```

TOP EXAM TIP

Wireless internet access is a major growth area. Make sure that you are familiar with WML tags and their functions.

26.

This question is about various aspects of the Internet, including search engines, web pages and e-commerce.

(a)   Search engines build their indexes by using web spiders or web crawlers. These are computer programs that browse the Web in a methodical fashion, creating a copy of all visited pages for subsequent indexing. (1 mark) A web spider normally starts from an initial list of URLs, known as the seeds. As the crawler visits these URLs, it identifies all the hyperlinks in the page and adds them to the list of URLs to be visited. (1 mark)

(b)   HTML tags can be used to format the text in an HTML page. Each tag must be explicitly terminated by repeating the tag, preceded by a slash (/).   (1 mark)

```
<html>
<body>

<h4>Options Available:</h4>
<ul>
  <li>Artificial Intelligence</li>
  <li>Computer Networking</li>
  <li>Multimedia Technology</li>
</ul>

</body>
</html>
```

The <body> tag indicates the start of the main body of the document   (1 mark)

The <h4> tag indicates the start of a Level 4 heading.   (1 mark)

The <ul> tag indicates the start of an unordered list.   (1 mark)

The <li> tag indicates the start of an element in a list   (1 mark)

TOP EXAM TIP

Questions about HTML tags frequently crop up in the Higher Computing exam, so you should be familiar with a range of tags and their functions.

(c)   E-commerce sites generally offer a much wider range of goods that are available in a bricks-and-mortar store (1 mark) and are often cheaper as they do not have the same storage or warehousing costs. (1 mark)

(d)   The Secure Sockets Layer (SSL) protocol can be used to set up a secure channel between the user's computer and a web server. (1 mark) Digital certificates can be used to verify the identity of users. (1 mark)

(e)   Individuals or communities are described as information-poor if they lack access to the equipment and network infrastructure required to access the internet. (1 mark)

27.

This question is about various aspects of Network Security, including protective techniques, types of attack content filtering and backup strategies.

(a)   Access to hardware can be controlled via physical security, such as keeping serves in a locked room, or by means of biometric security devices, such as iris scans or thumbprint readers. (1 mark) Access to data can be controlled by means of access rights for different groups of users or by setting permissions on files or folders. (1 mark)

(b)   Passive attacks involve spying on or stealing data. (1 mark) Active attacks attempt to modify or delete data or to cause a network to crash. (1 mark)

(c)   The following techniques can be used to carry out a DoS attack:
• Exploiting weaknesses in the server or operating system software. (1 mark)
• Flooding a server with a large number of data packets in a short period of time. (1 mark)
• Filling the cache on DNS servers with lookup information for non-existent hosts. (1 mark)

(d)   Internet content can be filtered by means of filtering software, which can filter by type of internet service, by URL, by checking for forbidden words or by content rating. (1 mark) It can also be filtered by means of a firewall which can be hardware or software based and can filter at the packet, circuit or application level. (1 mark)

(e)   Two backup strategies which allow access to be restored instantly include the use of a backup server, which can be used to replace the server on which the disk failed (1 mark) and the use of RAID or mirrored disks which would allow the failed disk to be replaced by an identical copy. (1 mark)

28.

This question is about various aspects of Data Transmission, particularly the TCP/IP protocol suite.

(a)   Asynchronous data transmission transmits single characters, preceded by one or more start bits and followed by one or more stop bits. (1 mark)

(b)   TCP is concerned with end-to-end communication, eg: between a browser and a Web server. (1 mark) It provides reliable, ordered delivery of a stream of bytes from a program on one computer to a program on another computer. (1 mark) It also controls message size, the rate at which messages are exchanged, and network traffic congestion. (1 mark)

TOP EXAM TIP

Make sure that you know how both Circuit Switching and Packet Switching work and the major differences between them.

(c)   Circuit switching requires a dedicated connection between two systems, lasting for the duration of the transmission. This is inefficient as the connection might be idle for long periods. Packet switching does not require a dedicated connection. (1 mark) As the name implies, packet switching involves splitting a message into discrete packets which may be transmitted from source to destination via different routes. This allows more efficient use of the available communications channels. (1 mark)

TOP EXAM TIP

Remember that TCP/IP isn't a single protocol. It's a suite consisting of two protocols, Transmission Control Protocol (TCP) and Internet Protocol (IP). You should be aware of the distinct functions carried out by each of these.

(d)   An ADSL connection offers the highest speed and the greatest bandwidth. (1 mark)

(e)   A cable connection would be best as it can be used for both cable TV and internet. (1 mark)

SECTION III
Part C – Multimedia Technology

29.

This question is about various aspects of creating a graphically-intensive multimedia application, using images captured with a digital camera.

(a)   The normal software development process applies in the same way to the development of multimedia applications as it does to traditional applications. (1 mark)

(b)   Authoring software can be used to link media elements of various different types (eg: text, audio, still images, video) together to form a coherent multimedia application. (1 mark) It will also offer facilities for capturing, editing and manipulating the different types of media, but these may be restricted in comparison to the facilities offered by standalone packages. (1 mark)

(c)   A digital camera uses CCDs instead of film. A CCD is basically a grid composed of microscopic light-sensitive cells. (1 mark) When light strikes the CCD, each sensor or pixel produces an electrical signal proportional to the intensity of light it receives. An image can be built up from this grid of pixels. (1 mark)

(d)   RGB colour codes use 8 bits (1 byte) to represent each of the colours red, green and blue. Primary colours are represented by having the relevant byte set to 255 and the others to 0 eg: red is (255, 0, 0). (1 mark) Secondary colours are represented by having 2 bytes set to 255, eg: Yellow (which is a combination of red and green) is (255, 255, 0). (1 mark) More complex colours are represented by the appropriate settings of all 3 bytes.

(e) $640 \times 480 \times 24 = 7372800$ bits (1 mark)

       $= 7372800/8 = 921600$ bytes

       $= 921600/1024 = 900$ megabytes. (1 mark)

(f)   (i)   Dithering is the process of creating additional colours from an existing palette by interspersing pixels of different colours. (1 mark)

       (ii)   Anti-aliasing is the process of smoothing the edges of graphics and text to prevent jagged edges. (1 mark)

       (iii)   Re-sampling is the process of increasing or reducing the number of pixels in an image, in order to change its resolution without altering its size. (1 mark)

TOP EXAM TIP

Make sure that you can define dithering, anti-aliasing and re-sampling and that you know the differences between them.

30.

This question is about various aspects of digital audio and MIDI files.

(a)   A sound card uses three major components to translate between analogue and digital data:

       • A Digital Signal Processor (DSP)

       • An analogue-to-digital converter (ADC)

       • A digital-to-analogue converter (DAC)   (1 mark)

       Analog sound data is input from a microphone or a direct connection to an analogue audio device. (1 mark) The DSP receives and handles the incoming sound signals. The ADC translates the analog waves into digital data that the computer can understand by sampling the sound, ie: taking precise measurements of the wave at frequent intervals. (1 mark) The faster a card's sampling rate, the more accurate the digitised audio. (1 mark)

(b)   When audio files are recorded some sounds can be louder or quieter than others. (1 mark) Normalising means adjusting the volume of the sounds to bring it closer to an average value. (1 mark) One application is that if an album has tracks at different volumes they can be normalised to make them all equal.

(c)   (i)   Clipping occurs when an attempt is made to record a sound at too high a level. The peak of the sound wave is flattened, leading to distortion in the sound. (1 mark)

       (ii)   Stereo is a method of reproducing sound, using two independent audio channels, through two loudspeakers or headphones, in order to create a more natural impression of sound coming from various directions. (1 mark)

       (iii)   Surround sound is an audio effect created by using multiple speakers powered by separate audio channels to simulate natural sound. (1 mark)

       (iv)   Fade is a gradual increase or decrease in the level of an audio signal. (1 mark)

(d)

       • Instrument: the MIDI instrument upon which the note is played.   (1 mark)

       • Pitch: the frequency of a note.   (1 mark)

       • Volume: the loudness (amplitude) of a note.   (1 mark)

       • Duration: the length of a note: (1 mark)

31.

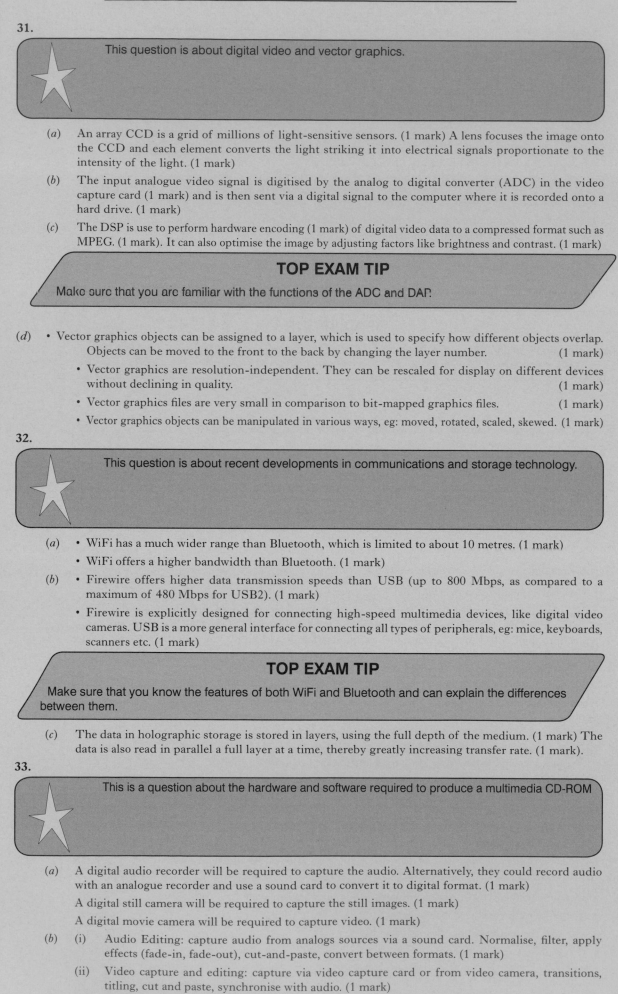

This question is about digital video and vector graphics.

(a) An array CCD is a grid of millions of light-sensitive sensors. (1 mark) A lens focuses the image onto the CCD and each element converts the light striking it into electrical signals proportionate to the intensity of the light. (1 mark)

(b) The input analogue video signal is digitised by the analog to digital converter (ADC) in the video capture card (1 mark) and is then sent via a digital signal to the computer where it is recorded onto a hard drive. (1 mark)

(c) The DSP is use to perform hardware encoding (1 mark) of digital video data to a compressed format such as MPEG. (1 mark). It can also optimise the image by adjusting factors like brightness and contrast. (1 mark)

TOP EXAM TIP

Make sure that you are familiar with the functions of the ADC and DAC.

(d) • Vector graphics objects can be assigned to a layer, which is used to specify how different objects overlap. Objects can be moved to the front to the back by changing the layer number. (1 mark)

• Vector graphics are resolution-independent. They can be rescaled for display on different devices without declining in quality. (1 mark)

• Vector graphics files are very small in comparison to bit-mapped graphics files. (1 mark)

• Vector graphics objects can be manipulated in various ways, eg: moved, rotated, scaled, skewed. (1 mark)

32.

This question is about recent developments in communications and storage technology.

(a) • WiFi has a much wider range than Bluetooth, which is limited to about 10 metres. (1 mark)

• WiFi offers a higher bandwidth than Bluetooth. (1 mark)

(b) • Firewire offers higher data transmission speeds than USB (up to 800 Mbps, as compared to a maximum of 480 Mbps for USB2). (1 mark)

• Firewire is explicitly designed for connecting high-speed multimedia devices, like digital video cameras. USB is a more general interface for connecting all types of peripherals, eg: mice, keyboards, scanners etc. (1 mark)

TOP EXAM TIP

Make sure that you know the features of both WiFi and Bluetooth and can explain the differences between them.

(c) The data in holographic storage is stored in layers, using the full depth of the medium. (1 mark) The data is also read in parallel a full layer at a time, thereby greatly increasing transfer rate. (1 mark).

33.

This is a question about the hardware and software required to produce a multimedia CD-ROM

(a) A digital audio recorder will be required to capture the audio. Alternatively, they could record audio with an analogue recorder and use a sound card to convert it to digital format. (1 mark)

A digital still camera will be required to capture the still images. (1 mark)

A digital movie camera will be required to capture video. (1 mark)

(b) (i) Audio Editing: capture audio from analogs sources via a sound card. Normalise, filter, apply effects (fade-in, fade-out), cut-and-paste, convert between formats. (1 mark)

(ii) Video capture and editing: capture via video capture card or from video camera, transitions, titling, cut and paste, synchronise with audio. (1 mark)

(iii) Bitmapped-graphics editing: rescale, resample, crop, apply effects. (1 mark)

(iv) Vector graphics: create and manipulate vector graphic elements (lines, shapes, text etc.) (1 mark)

SECTION I

1.

This question is about converting binary to decimal.

11	10	9	8	7	6	5	4	3	2	1	0
1	1	0	1	1	0	1	1	1	1	0	1

$2^{11} + 2^{10} + 2^8 + 2^7 + 2^5 + 2^4 + 2^3 + 2^2 + 2^0$

$2048 + 1024 + 256 + 128 + 32 + 16 + 8 + 4 + 1$

3517   (1 mark)

HINT   You might find it useful to draw up a table of the powers of 2 when converting binary to decimal.

2.

This is a question about converting from Megabytes (MB) to Terabytes (B). Remember that the factor involved is always 1024 (2^{10}) rather than 1000.

$60 \times 10000 = 600,000$ Megabytes

$600,000/1024 = 2929.69$ Gigabytes   (1 mark)

$2929.692929.69/1024 = / 1024 = 2.86$ Terabytes

2×2 Terabyte hard disks would be required.   (1 mark)

3.

This question is about the functions of the CPU registers.

The Instruction Register stores the instruction currently being executed. (1 mark)

The Program Counter stores the address of the next instruction to be executed. (1 mark)

The Accumulator holds the data currently being processed. (1 mark)

HINT   It is recommended that you become familiar with the functions of the Instruction Register, Program Counter and Accumulator.

4.

This question is about the difference between parallel and serial interfaces. PCs traditionally used a parallel Centronics interface to communicate with printers, but their use has declined significantly since the introduction of USB.

With a parallel interface multiple bits can be transferred simultaneously across a number of parallel wires. (1 mark) With a serial interface bits are transferred one at a time over a single wire. (1 mark)

5.

This question is about Computer Networks, in particular the difference between a network and a mainframe with terminals and the function of a Network Interface Card (NIC).

(*a*)   Terminals are dumb devices with no processing power, memory or backing storage of their own. Network workstations are intelligent devices with their own processor, memory and backing store. (1 mark)

In a mainframe system all the resources are concentrated in the central mainframe. In a network they can be distributed amongst the nodes and shared with other nodes. (1 mark)

(b)   A Network Interface Card (NIC) converts data stored on a computer into a format which can be transmitted over a network. (1 mark) Each NIC has a MAC (Media Access Centre) address which uniquely identifies the card. (1 mark)

6.

> This question is about the hardware and software facilities required to run particular applications.

The application may require particular hardware facilities (eg main memory (1 mark) or backing storage (1 mark)). It may also require a specific operating system. (1 mark)

7.

> This question is about documentation.

Good documentation is essential to allow end-users to make effective use of the software (1 mark) and to allow technical staff to install and maintain it.   (1 mark)

> **HINT**   Remember that the production of documentation is one of the stages of the Software Development Cycle.

8.

> This question is about the differences between compilers and interpreters.

An interpreter translates each line of a program into machine code and executes it immediately. This means that if a programmer makes a modification to a program he can run it immediately to see the effect of the modification, (1 mark) rather than having to wait for the whole program to be translated by a compiler. (1 mark)

TOP EXAM TIP

Make sure that you are clear about the differences between compilers and interpreters and the uses of each. This topic crops up frequently in the Higher Computing exam.

> **HINT**   Remember that interpreters are usually used for developing programs while compilers are used to create the final production version.

9.

> This question is about expressing the logic of a process in English-like pseudocode, then converting this to a high-level language.

(a)   Select Case Mark   (1 mark)
       Case "A"
          Print "Excellent"   (1 mark)
       Case "B"
          Print "Good"   (1 mark)
       Case "C"
          Print "Fair"   (1 mark)
       End Select

(b)   Case mark of   (1 mark)

       'A': Writeln('Excellent');   (1 mark)
       'B': Writeln('Good');
       'C': Writeln('Fair');
       End;

> **HINT**   Take care! Don't fall in to the trap of making your pseudocode too similar to a programming language.

> ## TOP EXAM TIP
> Make sure that you are familiar with the use of the CASE statement. This topic often appears in the Higher Computing exam.

10.

 This question is about the use of the standard algorithm for Counting Occurrences.

(a) The standard algorithm for Counting Occurrences. (1 mark)

(b) Let count = 0 (1 mark)

For index = 1 to items_in_list (1 mark)

    If height_table(index) > 1.80 then (1 mark)

        Let count = count + 1

End loop

Display count (1 mark)

> ## TOP EXAM TIP
> Make sure that you are familiar with the four standard algorithms: Counting Occurrences, Searching a List, Finding Minimum, Finding Maximum. The last two are really just variations on a single algorithm. In addition to being able to state the standard algorithms you must be able to apply them in new situations. One common extension is to take note of the location in a list at which something is found. This topic crops up frequently in the Higher Computing exam.

SECTION II

11.

This question is about various aspects of setting up a web site.

(a) A vector graphics image needs less storage space than a bit-mapped image. (1 mark)

A vector graphics image can be scaled to print/display on any suitable device without loss of resolution. (1 mark)

(b) Compressed images require less storage space. (1 mark)

(c) $512 \times 384 \times 24 = 4718592$ bits (1 mark)

$4718592/8 = 589824$ bytes

$589824/1024 = 576$ Kilobytes (1 mark)

> **HINT** Questions about selling up websites occur frequently in Higher Computing Exam papers. This is a common theme for drawing questions on different topics together and it is important that you fully understand the broad range of issues that can be involved.

(d) An interface is responsible for: buffering (1 mark), data format conversion (1 mark), voltage conversion (1 mark), protocol conversion (1 mark), handling of status signals (1 mark).

Note: any four of these answers would be acceptable.

(e) • Clock Speed: the number of clock cycles per second, measured in GHz. (1 mark)

• MIPS: Millions of Instructions Per Second, ie: the number of instructions that can be executed each second. (1 mark)

• FLOPS: Floating Point Operations Per Second, ie: the number of floating point operations that can be carried out each second. (1 mark)

• Application Based Tests: the speed with which specific application tasks can be completed. (1 mark)

> ## TOP EXAM TIP
> Remember to show your working in all calculations. If you do this, you may gain some marks, even if the final answer is wrong.

(f) Processor speeds are increasing (1 mark) and backing storage is becoming faster and cheaper (1 mark).

12.

This question is about various aspects of computer networks, including topology, software, legislation and viruses.

(a)

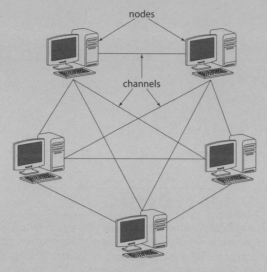

nodes

channels

Note: 1 Mark each for showing nodes, channels, and multiple connections between nodes.

(b) If a node goes down the remaining nodes will remain connected and continue to function. (1 mark) If a channel goes down all the nodes in the network remain connected, although it may be necessary in some cases for messages to pass through intermediate machines. (1 mark)

TOP EXAM TIP

Make sure that you can produce labeled diagrams of all the major network topologies: Bus, Ring, Star and Mesh. This appears frequently in the Higher Computing examination.

(c) Improvements in network operating systems (1 mark) and in network client software, such as browsers. (1 mark)

(d) The Data Protection Act. (1 mark)

TOP EXAM TIP

Make sure that you know the names of the major pieces of legislation that can apply to network users, particularly the Computer Misuse Act, The Data Protection Act, The Copyright, Designs and Patents Act and the Regulation of Investigatory Powers Act.

(e) Viruses are usually attached to an executable file and do not take effect until some human action, such as executing an infected file, is taken. They are spread by means of email attachments or by transferring files between computers and can corrupt or delete files. (1 mark)

Worms are similar to viruses but can travel between systems unaided. Worms may also corrupt or delete data or they may try to crash systems by consuming scarce resources. (1 mark)

Trojans are malicious programmes disguised as innocent looking applications. They are often used to create back doors, allowing hackers to enter systems. (1 mark)

TOP EXAM TIP

Make sure that you know the differences between viruses, worms and trojans.

(f) Virus Signature: viruses can often be detected by means of a virus signature, ie: a section of code that is recognised as belonging to a specific virus. (1 mark)

Checksum: a checksum is a sum created by some type of mathematical manipulation, such as treating each byte in a program as an integer and adding up their values. If the code has been amended due to infection by a virus this can be detected by recalculating the checksum. (1 mark)

Heuristic Detection: watches for suspicious behavior on the part of a program to see if it has been infected by a virus. (1 mark)

TOP EXAM TIP

Make sure that you know the about heuristic detection of viruses. Don't confuse this with other virus detection techniques, such as signatures or checksums.

13.

This question is about the software development cycle and the different types of programming language and their uses.

(a) The software specification is a document describing the functions the software is required to perform in order to meet the needs of the client. (1 mark) It often serves as the basis for the software development contract. (1 mark)

(b) Stepwise refinement is the process of breaking down a problem into sub-problems which can then be broken down into even smaller sub-problems (1 mark) until the stage is reached where the lowest-level problems can easily be solved by writing program code. (1 mark)

(c) Scripting languages are normally closely associated with a particular applications package. (1 mark) They allow an expert user to customise the use of the package (1 mark) and can be used to automate repetitive tasks. (1 mark)

TOP EXAM TIP

Make sure that you know the distinctive features of scripting languages.

(d) A macro is a sequence of instructions used to automate a task in an applications package. (1 mark) Macros can be hand-coded in a scripting language (1 mark) or they can be recorded as a series of steps, using the keyboard and the mouse, which is then converted into the scripting language. (1 mark)

(e) get forename

get deptname (1 mark)

firstpart = Left(forename, 5)

fastpart = Left(deptname, 5) (1 mark)

empcode = concat(forename, deptname) (1 mark)

14.

This question is about the different types of subprograms (subroutines and functions) and the differences between them.

(a) In Pascal the subroutine could be as follows:

```
procedure calcavg(invals: array of integer; var avg: real);    (1 mark)
var
     count, sum: integer;
begin
     sum := 0;
     for count := 0 to 9 do
          sum := sum + invals[count];
     avg := sum/10
end;                                                            (1 mark)
```

The declarations in the main program would be:
```
     values: array[0..9] of integer;
     average: real;
```

The subroutine would be called as follows:
```
     calcavg(values, average);                                  (1 mark)
```

(b) The user-defined function could be:
```
     function calcavg(invals: array of integer): real;          (1 mark)
     var
          count, sum: integer;
     begin
          sum := 0;
          for count := 0 to 9 do
               sum := sum + invals[count];
          calcavg := sum/10
     end;                                                       (1 mark)
```

The declarations in the main program would be as above. The function would be called as follows:
```
     average := calcavg(values);                                (1 mark)
```

(c) The scope of a variable is the area of a program in which the variable is visible. (1 mark) A global variable is visible throughout the whole program but a local variable is only visible within the subprogram in which it is declared. (1 mark)

15.

> This question is about using one of the standard algorithms, Finding Minimum. It includes the variation of finding where the minimum occurs.

(a)
```
let min = sunhours(1)                              (1 mark)
for count = 2 to 30 do                             (1 mark)
    if sunhours(count) < min then
        let min : sunhours(count)                  (1 mark)
    end if
end loop
display min                                        (1 mark)
```

(b)
```
begin
    min := sunhours[1];                            (1 mark)
    for count := 2 to 30 do                        (1 mark)
        if sunhours[count] < min then
            min := sunhours[count];                (1 mark)
    writeln('The minimum is: ', min:5:2)           (1 mark)
    end.
```

(c) This would require another pass through the array:
```
for count = 1 to 30 do
    if sunhours(count) = min then                  (1 mark)
        display (sunhours(count))                  (1 mark)
    end if
end loop
```

TOP EXAM TIP

Know your standard algorithms! They always crop up. Remember, you need to know how to apply them in an unfamiliar context as well as simply stating them.

SECTION III

Part A – Artificial Intelligence

16.

> This question is on various aspects relating to the development of artificial intelligence.

(a) The Turing test is regarded as flawed because it depends as much on the human interrogator as the machine. (1 mark) It uses a very limited language-based definition of intelligence and neglects other factors, such as cognitive and problem-solving abilities. (1 mark)

(b) Procedural language programs have a fixed start and end point and a defined route through them. Declarative language programs have no fixed start or end point. (1 mark) Declarative language programs consist of a collection of facts and rules. Procedural Language programs consist of a sequence of instructions for solving a problem. (1 mark)

TOP EXAM TIP

Games are an important application area for AI. You should be able to describe and give examples of the success and failures of game playing programs from simple early examples to contemporary complex examples exhibiting intelligence.

(c) Problems that can arise when applying artificial intelligence techniques to game playing include dealing with the complexity of the game rules (1 mark) and determining how moves should be evaluated to increase the chances of winning. (1 mark)

(d) The advantages of parallel processing include the ability to carry out multiple calculations simultaneously, decreasing the time required for calculation (1 mark) and the ability to follow alternative paths simultaneously, reducing the time needed to select the optimum move. (1 mark)

17.

This question covers three important applications of AI: computer vision, expert systems and intelligent software for controlling devices.

(a) Computer vision involves the following five stages:

- image acquisition: the initial capture of the image (1 mark)

- signal processing: conversion of the image into digital format (1 mark)

- edge detection: producing an outline of the image by determining where its edges are located (1 mark)

- object recognition: identifying the objects in the image by comparing them against other known objects (1 mark)

- image understanding: relating the objects in the image to one another to gain an understanding of the whole image (1 mark)

(b) Expert systems have the following advantages:

- expert systems are cheaper than using human experts (1 mark)
- expert systems are highly portable and can be used anywhere (1 mark)
- expert systems produce more consistent results than human experts (1 mark)
- multiple copies of an expert system can be used simultaneously (1 mark)

(c) Applications of intelligent software for controlling devices include:
- engine management systems which can determine when a car is due for a service
- traffic light control systems which can observe traffic flow patterns and make intelligent sequencing decisions
- fridge monitoring systems which can determine when stocks of food items are running low and produce reordering information.

18.

This question is about searching trees. You should know the difference between depth-first and breadth-first searches and be able to list the output from each.

(a) (i)   Alan, Angela, Morag, Bob, Hugh, Pat, Shirley, George, Hamish, Jeff, Mary, Robin, Ruth, Susan, Tony (1 mark)

(ii) Alan, Angela, Bob, George, Hamish, Hugh, Jeff, Mary, Morag, Pat, Robin, Ruth, Shirley, Susan, Tony (1 mark)

(b) A breadth-first search will find the solution in the fewest moves, (1 mark) but it requires more memory as the whole tree needs to be stored in memory. (1 mark)

(c) Combinatorial explosion occurs when the number of possible states in a system becomes unmanageable. (1 mark) For example if each node in a tree has two successors then the first level of the tree will have one node, the second level two nodes, the third level four nodes and so on. The number of nodes increases exponentially. By the time we reach the 10th level, there will be $2^{10} = 1024$ nodes. (1 mark)

19.

This question is about constructing a semantic net.

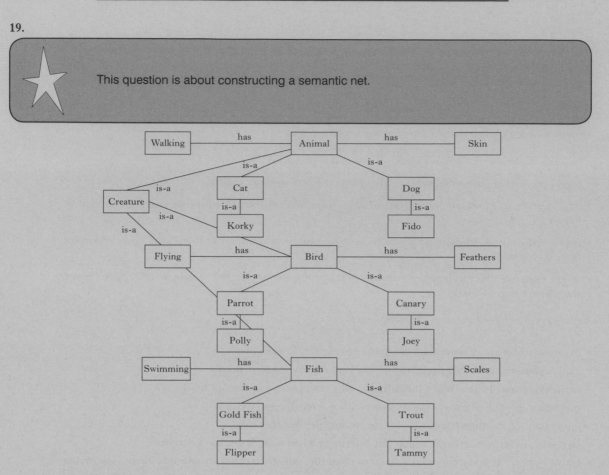

Note: 1 mark for each fact correctly recorded in diagram, to a maximum of 10.

20.

This question is about expressing a logic problem in Prolog.

(*a*) (i) mother(X, Y) :- parent(X, Y), female(X).   (1 mark)

       (ii) grandparent(A, B) :- parent(A, X), parent(X, B).   (1 mark)

(*b*) L15. A is instantiated to george. Goal becomes parent(george, B).

       L12. B is instantiated to peter.

       Goal is now matched. Output peter.

       Backtrack to L16. A is instantiated to george. First sub-goal becomes parent(george, X).

       L12. X is instantiated to peter.

       Backtrack to L16. X is instantiated to peter in first sub-goal.

       16 B is instantiated to mary.

       Backtrack to L15. A is instantiated to peter.

       L13 B is instantiated to mary.

       Backtrack to L16. X is instantiated to peter in second sub-goal.

       Both sub-goals are now matched. Output mary

SECTION III

Part B – Computer Networking

21.

This question is about various aspects of Computer Networking, including the OSI model, IP address classes, error detection and the CSMA/CD protocol.

(a)   The Physical Layer specifies the physical and electrical characteristics, such as type of cabling and voltage levels. (1 mark) Repeaters and hubs operate in this layer. (1 mark)

       The Data Link Layer organises bits into packets and is responsible determining the size and addressing of packets and for error checking, error correction and hardware addressing. (1 mark) Switches operate at this layer. (1 mark)

       The Network layer defines IP addresses and creates packet headers. It is responsible for routing packets between networks. (1 mark) Routers operate at this layer. (1 mark)

TOP EXAM TIP

Make sure that you are familiar with the functions of the seven layers of the OSI model as this topic crops up frequently in the Higher Computing examination.

(b)   Class A addresses are used for very large networks. The first octet specifies the address of the network and the remaining three specify the addresses of the hosts. (1 mark)

       Class B addresses are used for large networks. The first two octets specify the address of the network and the remaining two specify the addresses of the hosts. (1 mark)

       Class C addresses are used for small networks. The first three octets specify the address of the network and the remaining octet specifies the addresses of the hosts. (1 mark)

       Class D addresses are used for multicasting, ie: sending a message to a group of hosts simultaneously. (1 mark)

(c)   Parity Bits are used for error checking in asynchronous transmission. The first bit of each byte is used as a parity bit. In even parity each byte should have an even number of 1s. The parity bit is set to either 0 or 1 to ensure that this is the case. On receipt, the parity bit is again checked to ensure that the byte has not been corrupted during transmission. (1 mark)

TOP EXAM TIP

Make sure that you are familiar with the use of checksums for error detection. Remember, checksums also have other uses, eg: in the detection of computer viruses.

       Checksums are used for error checking in synchronous transmission. The content of each byte in a packed is treated as a numerical value. All the values in the packet are added to create a checksum which is stored in the packet. On receipt of the packet the checksum is recalculated to ensure that the packet has not been corrupted during transmission. (1 mark)

(d)   Carrier Sense Multiple Access/Collision Detect (CSMA/CD) is a network access protocol used to ensure that only one host in a network is transmitting data at any given time. If a host wishes to transmit data it checks that there is no other host already transmitting. If this is the case, it begins transmission. (1 mark) However there is always the possibility that two hosts will begin transmitting simultaneously. If this happens, the packets will collide, causing the content to be corrupted. (1 mark) If a collision is detected each of the transmitting hosts waits a different length of time before attempting retransmission. (1 mark)

TOP EXAM TIP

CSMA/CD crops up frequently in the Higher Computing Examination. Make sure that you can describe how it works and state its implications for network performance.

22.

       This question covers several topics in Computer Networking, including Networking Protocols, Search Engines, Ethical Implications and Legislation.

(a)   File Transfer Protocol (FTP) is used for transferring data from one computer to another over a network.

       HyperText Transfer Protocol (HTTP) is used for transferring web pages from a web server to a client.

       Simple Mail Transfer Protocol (SMTP) is used for transmitting email messages from a mail server.

       TELNET is used for logging on to remote systems as a terminal.

(b)   Search engine spiders crawl the net looking for pages to index in the search engine's database. (1 mark) They find pages from links on known web pages or from submissions from users. (1 mark) They record details of page titles, keywords and content and store these in the database, (1 mark) where users can find them by means of searches. (1 mark)

(c) Many people are concerned about the amount of information stored by ISPs about internet users and their activities, usually as a result of government legislation. They believe that this represents a threat to personal privacy and that personal information can be abused by advertisers to target individuals on the basis of their browsing habits. (1 mark) There are also concerns about employers monitoring the browsing habits of their employees or the emails they send and receive. (1 mark)

There are wide variations in opinion relating to Internet censorship. Almost everyone accepts that children and young people should be protected from objectionable content, but many people believe that adults should have the right to view any content they wish, unless it is illegal. (1 mark) Others believe that all content that might be objectionable to anyone should be blocked. In practice, this is difficult to control as many servers are located overseas and are not bound by UK law. (1 mark)

(d) The Regulation of Investigatory Powers Act, 2000 gives the Government the power to:

- Intercept communications (1 mark)
- Obtain communications data (1 mark)
- Set up intrusive surveillance (1 mark)
- Access encrypted data (1 mark)

  (Note: any two of the above would be acceptable).

23.

This question covers several aspects of Network Security.

(a) Data Integrity: all data stored on computer networks must be protected against loss or corruption. This is usually achieved by restricting access to the data and making regular backups. (1 mark)

Confidentiality: access to data should be restricted to those who have the right to view it. This is usually accomplished by the use of passwords and other forms of authentication. (1 mark)

Availability: the network should always be available to users. This is usually accomplished by taking steps to prevent damage by malicious individuals or programs and by having redundant backup systems. (1 mark)

(b) The following techniques can be used to carry out a Denial of Service (DoS) attack:

- Software Flaws: attackers can take advantage of previously-undiscovered flaws or loopholes in system software.
- Router Attacks: attackers can misuse router monitoring software to release malformed packets or redirect packets.
- Bandwidth consumption: attackers can flood the network with spurious traffic, causing servers to crash or making them unable to cope with legitimate users.
- Resource Starvation: attackers can consume resources other than bandwidth, eg: by filling the server's hard disk with spam emails.

(c) Firewalls can be used to prevent users from accessing certain web sites usually on the basis of IP address or protocol. (1 mark)

Internet Filtering Software can be used to restrict the sites that users can access, usually on the basis of type of content. (1 mark)

Walled Gardens can be used to give users access to only a limited part of the internet, normally by specifying the sites that can be accessed, rather than the sites that cannot be accessed. (1 mark)

TOP EXAM TIP

Firewalls crop up frequently in the Higher Computing Examination. You should be aware of the mechanisms by which a firewall protects, eg: port filtering, URL filtering, IP address filtering etc.

24.

This question is about several aspects of wireless networking, including types of wireless network, microbrowsers and WML.

(a) A Wireless Personal Area Network (WPAN) is a network which allows mobile devices such as PDAs, mobile phones and pagers to connect to each other and to nearby stationary devices such as PCs and printers. (1 mark) The technology used is Bluetooth, which can link over a range of about 10 metres with a maximum speed of 780 kbps. (1 mark)

A Wireless Local Area Network (WLAN) is one in which network devices are linked via wireless signals rather than cables. They were originally slower than cabled LANs, but speeds are increasing rapidly. (1 mark) The clients on a wireless LAN communicate with an access point, which is linked to a server. (1 mark)

A Wireless Wide Area Network (WWAN) is one based on wireless connections rather than cables. Three different types of links are in use: mobile telephone links, satellite links and mobile broadband. (1 mark) Mobile telephone links are slow and expensive and satellite links can be very expensive, as well as often needing a landline connection for uploads. Mobile broadband is becoming increasingly popular and provides a good balance between cost and speed. (1 mark)

(b) Microbrowsers often display text only and seldom display pages in the format originally intended by the owner of the website. (1 mark) They can have difficulty in displaying pages correctly if they are already formatted for display on a mobile device. (1 mark)

(c) WML (Wireless Markup Language) is similar to HTML. It uses tags to format pages for display on wireless devices. (1 mark) WML deals mostly with text and avoids the use of tags that would slow down communication with handheld devices. The use of tables and images is restricted. (1 mark) WML pages are known as decks and are composed of linked pages. When a deck is accessed from a mobile device, all the cards in the page are downloaded from the WAP server. Navigation between the pages takes place within the device, without further visits to the server. (1 mark)

TOP EXAM TIP

You should be familiar with the use of WML to layout web pages for display on mobile devices.

SECTION III
Part C – Multimedia Technology

25.

> This question is about the JPEG graphics format and graphics cards.

(a) The JPG format should be used to store the images. (1 mark) This is the best format for photographs and the page images will be very similar to photographs. (1 mark)

(b) $10 \times 8 \times 200 \times 24 = 384000$ bits   (1 mark)

$384000/8 = 48000$ bytes

$48000/1024 = 46.875$ kilobytes   (1 mark)

(c) The Graphics Processing Unit (GPU) is responsible for handling the following aspects of 3D graphics:

- Rotation: viewing 3D objects from different angles (1 mark)
- Translation: moving 3D objects to different locations (1 mark)
- Scaling: changing the size of 3D objects (1 mark)
- Rendering: lighting and shading 3D objects (1 mark)

26.

> This question assesses your familiarity with various aspects of digital audio.

(a) Streamed audio is broken down into packets so it can start playing as soon as the first packet has arrived, rather than having to wait for the entire audio file to be downloaded, as happens with embedded audio. (1 mark)

(b) A codec (coder-decoder) is a device or program that can encode or decode a digital data stream or signal, such as a music or video file. (1 mark)

(c) A container file is one that holds several compressed files, for example, media files and the corresponding codecs, allowing them to be transferred over a network in a single operation. (1 mark)

(d) MP3 aims to compress a CD-quality song without noticeably affecting sound quality, allowing songs to be downloaded more rapidly and use less storage. (1 mark) MP3 uses a technique known as "perceptual noise shaping" which is based on the fact that the human ear hears some sounds louder than others and cannot hear some sounds at all. (1 mark) Thus some parts of a song can be eliminated without noticeably reducing the sound quality. The remainder of the song can then be compressed by a factor of around 10, using a technique known as Huffman encoding. (1 mark)

(e) ADPCM stands for Adaptive Delta Pulse Code Modulation.   (1 mark)

(f) ADCPM is applied to files that are already stored in PCM format. It stores the changes between successive samples rather than storing the samples themselves (1 mark), as is the case with PCM. ADCPM files are about a quarter of the size of the corresponding PCM file. (1 mark)

(g) $2 \times 2 \times 44.1 \times 1000 \times 2 = 352800$ bytes (1 mark)

minutes   channels   samples   bit depth

(in bytes)

$352800/1024 = 344.53125$ megabytes   (1 mark)

(h) The DSP is used to compress and decompress sound files (1 mark) and to add effects, such as echo or reverb.   (1 mark)

27.

> This is a question about various aspects of digital video and display and storage technology.

(a) Several different techniques can be used to compress video files. Intraframe compression compresses each individual frame, using a lossy technique such as JPEG. (1 mark) Interframe compression stores only key frames (normally every 10th or 15th frame) and the changes between these and subsequent frames. (1 mark)

Additional techniques, including reducing bit depth, (1 mark) reducing frame rate, (1 mark) reducing resolution (1 mark) and cropping (1 mark) can be applied to further reduce the size of the final file. (*Note: any two of these would be acceptable.*)

(b) Sound can be incorporated into video files by using AVI (Audio Video Interleave). (1 mark) AVI files can store both audio and video data in a file container that allows synchronous audio-with-video playback. (1 mark)

(c) $320 \times 240 \times 24 \times 30 = 55296000$ bits   (1 mark)

$55296000/8 \qquad = 6912000$ bytes

$6912000/1024 \qquad = 6750$ kilobytes

$6750/1024 \qquad = 6.59$ megabytes   (1 mark)

(d) Firewire has a faster sustained data transfer speed than USB 2.0. (1 mark)

(e) Virtual 3D displays make use of virtual-reality headset, which has two monitors showing a different perspective for each eye. (1 mark) Real 3D displays illuminate points within a 3D space by means of rotating display panels or multi-planar displays. (1 mark)

(f) Holographic storage has a much greater storage capacity as data can be stored through the full depth of the medium, rather than just on the surface. (1 mark) Access speed is very rapid as millions of bits can be written or read in parallel. (1 mark)

TOP EXAM TIP

Make sure that you are familiar with holographic storage as it frequently crops up in the Higher Computing Examination.

28.

> This question is about MIDI music and 2D vector graphics.

(a) Notes stored as MIDI data have the following attributes:
- Instrument: the musical instrument being simulated flute, violin etc.) – represented as a MIDI instrument number. (1 mark)
- Pitch: the frequency of the note. (1 mark)
- Volume: the loudness of the note. (1 mark)
- Duration: the length of the note. (1 mark)
- Tempo: the rate at which notes are played, in beats per minute. (1 mark)

(b) Advantages:
- MIDI data files are much smaller than digitised audio files. (1 mark)
- Individual notes can easily be edited. (1 mark)

Disadvantages

- MIDI sound is not as realistic as digitised audio. (1 mark)
- MIDI cannot handle vocals. (1 mark)

(c) 2D vector graphic images have the following attributes:
- shape: the form of the image, eg: circle, rectangle, irregular etc. (1 mark)
- position: where the image is located on the screen. (1 mark)
- size: how large the image is. (1 mark)
- rotation: the orientation of the image. (1 mark)
- line: the characteristics of the lines making up the image, eg, weight, dotted etc. (1 mark)
- fill: colour, shading etc. of the area within the image. (1 mark)

(d) SVG (Scalable Vector Graphics) is a set of specifications for XML-based file formats for describing 2D vector graphics. (1 mark)

VRML (Virtual Reality Modeling Language) is a standard file format for representing 3D interactive vector graphics. (1 mark)

PRACTICE EXAM C   WORKED ANSWERS

SECTION I

1.

This question is about the range of numbers that can be stored in a memory location with a given number of bits.

The range 0 to 65535 can be stored in 16 bits. (1 mark)

HINT Remember, if a location is X bits wide, the range of numbers that can be stored is $2^X - 1$.

2.

This questions is about the two's complement representation of signed binary integers. A binary integer can be converted to two's complement by inverting the bits, ie: changing all the zeroes to ones and vice versa, and adding one.

128	64	32	16	8	4	2	1	
0	1	1	1	0	0	1	1	**115**
1	0	0	0	1	1	0	0	**Flip 0s and 1s** (1 mark)
						+	1	**Add 1**
1	0	0	0	1	1	0	1	**−115** (1 mark)

3.

This question is about the different types of memory to be found in a computer system.

(a) Registers are used to store data, addresses and instructions within the CPU. (1 mark)

(b) Cache is an area of fast memory which sits between the CPU and the main memory. It is used to improve the speed of access to items held in main memory. (1 mark)

(c) Main memory is used to store the programs currently being executed by the system and the data currently being processed. (1 mark)

HINT When answering questions about differing types of computer system memory you should ensure that you are familiar with the functions of main memory, cache memory and registers.

4.

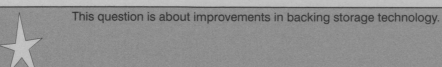

This question is about improvements in backing storage technology.

Backing storage devices are continuing to increase in capacity (1 mark) and access speeds are improving. (1 mark)

5.

This question is about the differences between Local Area Networks (LANs) and Wide Area Networks (WANs).

A LAN is usually confined to a fairly restricted geographical area, such as a single building or site. The machines are connected by copper cables or wireless connections. (1 mark)

A WAN covers a wide geographical area. Long-distance links between systems are generally telecommunications links and can involve microwave or satellite links or fibre-optic cables. (1 mark)

6.

This question is about the legislation relating to the use of computer networks.

(a)   Computer Misuse Act. (1 mark)

(b)   Copyright, Designs and Patents Act. (1 mark)

TOP EXAM TIP

Make sure that you are familiar with the names and provisions of the major legislation relating to the use of computer. This includes the Regulation of Investigatory Powers Act and the Data Protection Act in addition to the two Acts mentioned above.

7.

This question is about graphics file formats. Make sure that you are familiar with the details of all the major graphics file formats.

• JPG/JPEG (Joint Photographic Experts Group) (1 mark)
• GIF (Graphics Interchange Format) (1 mark)
• PNG (Portable Network Graphics) (1 mark)

Note: *other widely-used graphics file formats such as TIFF or BMP would also be acceptable.*

8.

This question is about approaches / techniques used in designing computer programs. The basic approach is derived from "divide and conquer".

"Top-Down Design" is the process of starting with a high-level statement of a problem and breaking it down into a series of smaller sub-problems. Each of these sub-problems can then be broken down into even smaller problems, until the stage is reached where the lower-level problems can easily be solved, eg: by coding them in a programming language. (1 mark)   "Stepwise refinement" is another name for the same process. (1 mark)

9.

This question is about the difference between compilers and interpreters. Ensure that you are thoroughly familiar with the differences between compilers and interpreters and the circumstances in which they are used.

A compiler translates a whole program into machine code before executing it. (1 mark) An interpreter translates it line-by-line, executing each line as soon as it is translated. (1 mark)

10.

> This question is about the uses of different data types in computer programs. Remember that integers are used for whole number, reals for numbers with a fractional part, strings for non-numeric data and 1d arrays for groups of data items of the same type.

(*a*)   Integer. (1 mark)

(*b*)   Real. (1 mark)

(*c*)   String. (1 mark)

(*d*)   1D array of real. (1 mark)

11.

> This question is about the use of built-in functions in high-level programming languages.

(*a*)   A built-in function is a pre-written subprogram for carrying out a specified task, for example calculating the square root of a number.

(*b*)   The substring function (eg: SUBSTR) is used to extract a substring of characters from a string, often from the beginning, middle or end. (1 mark)

The concatenation function (eg: CONCAT is used to concatenate or join together two strings into a single string. (1 mark)

(*Either of the above answers would be acceptable.*)

TOP EXAM TIP

String handling functions crop up frequently in the Higher Computing examination. You should be familiar with the use of functions for joining (concatenating) strings and extracting characters from strings in both pseudocode and a high-level language.

12.

> This question is about the Linear Search algorithm, used for locating an item in a list.

(*a*)   The Linear Search algorithm. (1 mark)

(*b*)   Assuming the number of items in the table is known, the algorithm would be as follows:

```
get (target)
let counter = 0                                        (1 mark)
do
    let counter = counter + 1                          (1 mark)
    if table(counter) = target then
        output target and counter                      (1 mark)
loop until counter = number of items in table          (1 mark)
```

TOP EXAM TIP

Make sure that you are familiar with the standard algorithms: Linear Search, Finding Occurrences and Finding Minimum/Maximum. You should be able to express these in both pseudocode and a high-level language and be able to apply them to solve problems, rather than simply stating them. One or more of these algorithms almost always appears in the Higher Computing examination.

SECTION II

13.

> The first two parts about this question are about techniques used for storing characters, bit-mapped and vector graphics.

(a)   Unicode uses a 16-bit representation, rather than the 8 bits used by ASCII. This allows many more characters to be represented, including foreign language characters. (1 mark)

(b)   Vector graphics require much less storage than bit-mapped graphics. (1 mark)

Vector graphics are scalable, so they can take advantage of the maximum resolution available on any device they are displayed on. (1 mark)

Bit-mapped graphics can become distorted (pixelated) when enlarged. Vector graphics do not have this problem. (1 mark)

Individual objects can be separated for editing in vector graphics. (1 mark)

The next two parts of this question are about the Software Development Process. You should be able to explain all the stages in the process and describe the roles of all the staff involved.

(c)   The software development process is iterative in the sense that earlier stages many need to be revisited as a result of information discovered at a later stage. (1 mark) For instance, if an error encountered at the testing stage is found to be due to a flaw in the design then the design and implementation stages would need to be revisited to correct it. (1 mark)

TOP EXAM TIP

You may be asked questions about the software development process in the context of non-traditional software development, such as the use of declarative languages, or the development of multimedia applications. The same software development process still applies, but is tailored to fit the circumstances.

(d)   The software specification states which tasks the software is required to carry out in order to meet the client's requirement. It often serves as the basis for a legally-binding contract. (1 mark)

The following three parts of this question are about various aspects of programming languages.

(e)   Procedural languages use a clearly defined set of instructions, with a specific path through them, to solve a given problem. (1 mark)

Declarative languages use queries to interrogate a knowledge base describing the problem area. (1 mark)

Event-driven languages respond to events in the external environment, such as key-presses or mouse clicks. There is no fixed path through the program as the path followed will depend on the events that occur. (1 mark)

(f)   Scripting languages are normally used for writing macros. (1 mark)

(g)   Programmers can save time by using pre-written routines from module libraries, rather than having to write them from scratch. (1 mark)

14.

This question is about various topics related to computer networks, computer hardware and systems software.

(a)

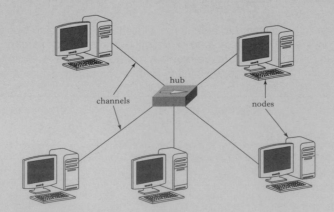

Note: One mark each for showing nodes, channels and hub.

(b)

    (i)   The ALU (Arithmetic and Logical Unit) is responsible for carrying out calculations and comparisons. (1 mark)

    (ii)   The Control Unit is responsible for coordination the activities of the other elements of the CPU. (1 mark)

    (iii) The Data Bus is used for transferring data between the CPU and the main memory. (1 mark)

    (iv) The address bus stores the address of the data currently being processed. (1 mark)

(c)   Cache memory speeds up the operation of the system. In general, the bigger the cache memory, the faster the system will be. (1 mark)

(d)   "Spooling" means storing the print files sent from the different nodes on the network on the print server's backing storage until the printer is free to print them. (1 mark) It is necessary because the printer takes much longer to print a document than the time required to transmit the document from the node to the print server. (1 mark)

(e)   Data is transferred over a serial interface 1 bit at a time. (1 mark) A parallel interface consists of multiple lines, so multiple bits can be transferred simultaneously. (1 mark) The most common parallel interface found on printers is the Centronics interface. (1 mark) The most common serial interface found nowadays is the USB (Universal Serial Bus) interface. (1 mark)

(f)   The use of wireless connections is increasing because of improvements in speed (1 mark) and security (1 mark).

15.

This question is about utility programs and viruses. Make sure that you are familiar with the various types of utility programs available, and the different types of malware, including viruses, trojans and worms.

(a)   Anti-virus software: used to prevent and or remove malware infections. (1 mark)

    Disk defragmenter: used to recover wasted disk space and improve disk performance by recombining fragmented files (1 mark)

    File Compression: used to minimise use of disk space by compressing files. (1 mark)

    Backup/Restore: used to create and restore security copies of critical files. (1 mark)

(b)   A virus is a piece of malicious code that is normally loaded onto a computer system without the user's knowledge. Viruses attack a system by attaching themselves to an executable program or to the boot sector and can corrupt other files by replicating. (1 mark)

    A worm is a piece of code that propagates itself across a computer network. It may perform malicious actions but often simply reduces network performance by wasting resources. (1 mark)

    A trojan is a malicious program that disguises itself as a benign application, often with the intention of allowing hackers access to the system. Unlike viruses, trojans do not replicate themselves. (1 mark)

(c)   Some utility programs might require a particular operating system, or specific hardware facilities, such as amount of main memory or backing storage. (1 mark)

16.

The first part of this question is about the use of the Case statement (or similar) for programming complex selections. Make sure you are familiar with this and can demonstrate the use of Case statements in both pseudocode and a high-level language. Professional programmers will virtually always use a Case statement in preference to nested if-statements to carry out complex selections.

(a)
```
Get month
Case month of                                    (1 mark)
    1 : Display "January"                        (1 mark)
    -------------------
    12 : Display "December"
End case                                          (1 mark)
```

(b)
```
procedure printmon(mon: integer);                (1 mark)
begin
    case mon of                                  (1 mark)
        1 : writeln('January');
        {code for remaining months}
        12 : writeln('December')
    End                                          (1 mark)
end;
```

The remainder of the question is about subprograms and parameter passing. Make sure that you are familiar with the differences between procedures and user defined functions and have a thorough grasp of the different parameter passing mechanisms (call-by-reference and call-by-value) and the circumstances in which each should be used.

(c)   A function returns a single value via the function name (1 mark). A procedure does not return values, but can change the values of variables passed as parameters using call-by-reference. (1 mark)

(d)   Modularity allows a program to be split up into a number of discrete chunks, each of which carries out a single function. This simplifies program design and makes maintenance easier as often only a single module requires modification. (1 mark)

(e)   With call-by-value, only a copy of the value of a variable is passed to the subprogram, so the variable itself cannot be altered within the subprogram. (1 mark) With call-by-reference, the location where the variable is stored is passed to the subprogram and changes to the value of the variable can be made within the subprogram. (1 mark)

17.

This question is about using the standard algorithm for finding the maximum value in a list. You should be familiar with the standard algorithms: Linear Search, Finding Occurrences and Finding Minimum/Maximum. You should be able to express these in both pseudocode and a high-level language and be able to apply them to the solution of problems, rather than simply stating them.

(a)   Remember to set the variable "highest" to a low value initially

```
    highest := 0;                                              (1 mark)
loop count from 1 to 31                                        (1 mark)
    if rain(count) > highest then
        highest = rain(count)                                  (1 mark)
        highday = count                                        (1 mark)
    endif
  end loop
display "The highest rainfall was :  ", highest, " on day:  ", highday
                                                               (1 mark)
```

(b)   There is no need to keep a note of the day upon which the highest rainfall occurred, but an additional loop through the array is needed after the highest value is known in order to display all the days on which it occurred.

If it is possible for the highest level of rainfall to occur on more than one day, then, as the algorithm stands, only the first day when that level occurred would be printed. (1 mark) To print all the days when the highest level occurred, the algorithm would need to be amended as follows:

```
highest = 0
loop count from 1 to 31                                        (1 mark)
    if rain(count) > highest then
        highest = rain[count]                                  (1 mark)
    endif
end loop
display "The highest rainfall was : "
display "It occurred on the following days: "
loop count from 1 to 31                                        (1 mark)
    if rain(count) = highest then
        display count                                          (1 mark)
    endif
end loop
```

SECTION III

Part A – Artificial Intelligence

18.

This question is about the characteristics of intelligent behaviour.

(a)   The following are important characteristics of intelligent behaviour:

• The ability to communicate by means of language. (1 mark)

• The ability to learn and adapt. (1 mark)

• The ability to collate information and draw conclusions (cognitive ability). (1 mark)

- The ability to apply existing knowledge to new situations (problem-solving). (1 mark)
- The ability to store and recall information (memory). (1 mark)
- The ability to be inventive and imaginative (creativity). (1 mark)

Note: any four of these responses would be sufficient.

 This question is about the use of AI techniques in game-playing programs.

(b) Difficulties can exist in the following areas when developing AI programs to play games:

- Representing the current state of the game, eg: where all the pieces are on a board. (1 mark)

- Defining the rules of the game in a programmable form. (1 mark)

- Keeping track of the possible moves for several steps ahead. (1 mark)

- Evaluating the extent to which alternative moves are likely to contribute towards an eventual win. (1 mark)

This question is about depth-first and breadth-first searching. You should be able to state the results of carrying out both types of search on a tree and the advantages and disadvantages of each.

(c)

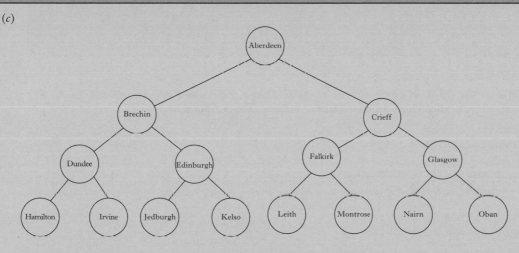

(i) If the nodes are visited in breadth-first order the names of the towns will be encountered as follows:

Aberdeen, Brechin, Crieff, Dundee, Edinburgh, Falkirk, Glasgow, Hamilton, Irvine, Jedburgh, Kelso, Leith, Montrose, Nairn, Oban. (1 mark)

If the nodes are visited in depth-first order the names of the towns will be encountered as follows:

Aberdeen, Brechin, Dundee, Hamilton, Irvine, Edinburgh, Jedburgh, Kelso, Crieff, Falkirk, Leith, Montrose, Glasgow Nairn, Oban. (1 mark)

(ii) The breadth-first approach requires the most memory as the whole tree needs to be stored in memory. (1 mark) The depth first approach requires less memory as only the branch currently being traversed needs to be stored and once the traversal is complete it can be discarded. (1 mark)

(iii) Backtracking only occurs with the depth-first search. If the goal has not been found by the end of a branch it is necessary to backtrack to the node where the last branching decision was made and choose an alternative branch to search. (1 mark)

19.

This question is about applications of AI including neural nets, Natural Language Processing (NLP) and intelligent robots.

(a) A neural net has four components: artificial neurons, links between these neurons, the weights allocated to the links and layers which generate signals. Learning takes place by an iterative method. (1 mark) Estimated weights are initially allocated to the links and test data is input. If the expected results are not obtained the weights are modified. This process continues until the expected results are obtained. (1 mark)

(b) Neural nets can be implemented by either software or hardware. Software nets are essentially specialised computer programs. (1 mark) Hardware neural nets employ special-purpose electronic components. (1 mark)

(c) Natural Language Processing (NLP) is used for the following applications:

- Machine translation (eg: Google Translate). (1 mark)

- Voice recognition (eg: Dragon Naturally Speaking). (1 mark)

- Natural language search engines (eg: Ask). (1 mark)

- Natural Language User interfaces (eg: GPS systems). (1 mark)

(d) Practical problems can be encountered when constructing intelligent robots include the following:

- Need for a mobile power supply (1 mark)

- Mobility problems (1 mark)

- Vision recognition (1 mark)

- Navigation and path planning (1 mark)

(any three would be acceptable)

These problems are gradually being overcome as technology improves eg: faster processors, more and faster memory), programming languages improve and programmers gain more experience.

20.

> This question is about various characteristics of declarative languages, including multi-argument clauses, recursive rules, multiple-variable queries, negation and inheritance.

(a) (i)   Multi-argument clauses

Imagine the situation where we wish to create a name, capital and language of each of the EU countries. We could have separate clauses for each item of information, eg:

```
country(france)
country(spain)
...
language(france, french)
language(spain spanish)
...
capital(france, paris)
capital(spain, madrid)
---
```

Our knowledge base would be quite large by the time we had included all the countries in the EU. We can simplify the knowledge base by using multi-argument clauses, eg:

```
country(france, french, paris)
country(spain, spanish, madrid)
```

This certainly makes the knowledge bases simpler, but it is also harder to read.

(ii)   Recursive rules

The following code shows a recursive definition of ancestor:

```
parent(john,malcolm).        /* malcolm is john's parent */
parent(malcolm,david).       /* david is malcolm's parent */
parent(david,mary).          /* mary is david's parent */

ancestor(X,Y) :- parent(X,Y).

/* If Y is a parent of X, then Y is an ancestor of X */

ancestor(X,Y) :- parent(X,Z), ancestor(Z,Y).

/* if Y is an ancestor of Z and Z is a parent of X,
then Y is an ancestor of X */
```
(1 mark)

Queries can now be run using this function, eg:

```
| ?- ancestor(john,david).
yes
| ?- ancestor(david,john).
No
```
(1 mark)

(iii)   Multiple variable queries

Imagine we have the following knowledge base giving details of family relationships:

```
female(tamara).
female(shirley).
male(bob).
male(len).
parent(bob, tamara).
parent(shirley,tamara).
```

We want to find out who Tamara's mother is, but the knowledge base has no concept of "mother". However, we know that a mother is a parent who is female. We can express this by means of a complex query. Complex queries need two or more conditions to be true. (1 mark) The conditions are separated by a comma in the query. The following query should give the correct answer:

?parent(X,tamara),female(X)   **(1 mark)**

(iv)   Negation

We can reduce the number of rules in a Prolog program if a rule can be stated as a negation of a fact, eg:

```
female(mary).
male(X) :- not female(X).
```

If we now submit the query male(mary) we get the expected result:

```
| ?- male(mary).
No
```
                                                        (1 mark)

However, if we submit the query male(shirley) the result seems strange:

```
| ?- male(shirley).
yes
```

This happens because the Prolog interpreter assumes that the database is a closed world. If it cannot prove something is true, it assumes that it is false. This is called negation as failure, ie: something is false if Prolog cannot prove it true, given the facts and rules in its database. (1 mark)

(v)   Inheritance

We sometimes need some kind of rule that allows us to state that if X is a member of a particular group then X should inherit all the properties of that group. This can be accomplished by the following recursive rule:

```
has(X,Y) :- is_a(X,G), has(G,Y)
```
                                                        (1 mark)

This means X has Y if X is in group G and G has Y. For example, Polly has feathers if Polly is a bird and birds have feathers. (1 mark)

(b)

This question is about the execution of queries in a declarative language such as Prolog.

(i)   Goal

A goal is whatever we are looking to find in a Prolog query, (1 mark) for example if the query is

```
parent(X, tamara)
```

The goal is to find a value for X which is a parent of Tamara. (1 mark)

(ii)   Sub-goal

Sometimes a goal can be made up of two or more sub-goals. (1 mark) For example, if we had the following facts and rule:

```
female(shirley)
parent(shirley, tamara)
mother(Mum, Child) :- female(Mum),
                      parent(Mum, Child).
```

then the goal for mother () has two sub-goals, female () and parent(). (1 mark)

(iii)   Instantiation

Instantiation means that an instance has been found during a search where a rule or a fact has a value. (1 mark) Eg: using the knowledge base given immediately above, Mum would be instantiated to "shirley" and Child would be instantiated to "tamara". (1 mark)

(c) Matching

    (i)   X = anne ;

        X = john ; (1 mark)

        X = george ;

        X = michael (1 mark)

    (ii)

        L16. Query geek(X) begins execution. (1 mark)
        L13. Query socialiser(X) begins execution. (1 mark)
        L1. X is instantiated to john
        L14. Query blogger(X) begins execution (1 mark)
        L6. Match found for john
        L13. Query gamer(X) begins execution (1 mark)
        L12. Match found for john
        Output john (1 mark)

SECTION III

Part B – Computer Networking

21.

This question is about various aspects of computer networking including the OSI Model, networking protocols and the Domain Name Service (DNS).

(a) The Application Layer handles specific applications, such as file transfer or mail transfer. (1 mark) It controls how applications communicate with the network. (1 mark)

The Presentation Layer translates application-specific data formats into a form suitable for transfer over the network. (1 mark) It also handles encryption and compression. (1 mark)

TOP EXAM TIP

Make sure that you are familiar with all seven layers of the OSI model and can describe the function of each layer briefly.

The Session Layer determines how connections between computers are initiated, maintained and terminated (1 mark) and synchronises the transfer of data over the network. (1 mark)

The Transport Layer breaks messages up into packets and reassembles these at the remote end. (1 mark) It also issues acknowledgements and retransmits packets. (1 mark)

(b)

Protocol Name	Function
TELNET (1 mark)	Logging on remotely to a server.
HTTP	Transmitting web pages from a server to a client. (1 mark)
FTP (1 mark)	Uploading and downloading files from a server
SMTP	Transmitting outgoing email messages from a mail server. (1 mark)

(c) The Domain Name Service (DNS) is used to convert user-friendly URLs (eg: www.google.com) to numeric IP addresses (eg: 209.85.171.100). (1 mark) It can also carry out the same function in reverse. (1 mark)

TOP EXAM TIP

Make sure that you can describe the function of the Domain Name Service (DNS) and the relationship between URLs and IP addresses.

22.

This question is about Network Applications, including HTML and e-commerce.

(a) The `<html>` tag indicates the start of the HTML code. (1 mark) It is terminated by the `</html>` tag. (1 mark)

The <head> tag indicates the start of the head section which defines details such as the title of the page. (1 mark) It is terminated by the </head> tag. (1 mark)

The <title> tag defines the title of the page. (1 mark) It is terminated by the </title> tag. (1 mark)

The <body> tag indicates the start of the main body of the page. (1 mark) It is terminated by the </body> tag. (1 mark)

The <h1> tag indicates the start of a Level 1 headline. (1 mark) It is terminated by the </h1> tag. (1 mark)

The <p> tag indicates the start of a paragraph. (1 mark) It is terminated by the </p> tag. (1 mark)

Note: any two of the above would be sufficient.

TOP EXAM TIP

Make sure that you are familiar with the use of HyperText Markup Language (HTML) to code web pages and that you can describe the functions of the principal HTML tags.

(*b*)   The advantages of e-commerce include the following:

- The retailer has access to a huge, world-wide customer base. (1 mark)
- There is no need for expensive premises and staff. (1 mark)
- The retailer can offer a far wider range than any bricks-and-mortar store. (1 mark)

Disadvantages include the following:

- E-commerce retailers can appear impersonal in comparison with real-life stores. (1 mark)
- Customers need to wait some time for delivery. (1 mark)
- Problems can arise if after-sales service is required. (1 mark)

(*c*)   The incidence of fraud can be minimised by using secure networking technologies, such as HTTPS (1 mark) or SET (1 mark) and by using third-party payment systems, such as PayPal.

(*d*)   There is considerable disagreement about effect that increased use of e-commerce is likely to have on employment. (1 mark) Some people believe that it will lead to a loss of jobs, because it will cause high-street stores to close. (1 mark) However, others believe that the new jobs created by e-commerce businesses will far outweigh the number lost. (1 mark)

23.

This question is about Network Security, including Denial of Service (DoS) attacks, firewalls and backup strategies.

(*a*)   Customers will be unable to access the company's servers. (1 mark) They will either have crashed, or be so slow to respond that transactions become almost impossible. (1 mark)

(*b*)   The company is likely to incur costs due to the loss of business during the attack (1 mark) and the cost of repairing systems and responding to the attack. (1 mark)

(*c*)   There can be a variety of reasons behind a DoS attack. Attacks may be carried out by disgruntled ex-employees, wanting to "get back" at the company, (1 mark) or they may be carried out for political reasons, eg: because the company is perceived as being environmentally unfriendly. (1 mark)

(*d*)   Firewalls can protect computer systems as follows:

- By filtering on IP address, ie: only allowing systems with specified IP addresses to access the network
(1 mark)

- By preventing access to the system via specified ports   (1 mark)

- By inspecting incoming packets for any suspicious signs (stateful packet inspection)   (1 mark)

TOP EXAM TIP

Make sure that you can describe the mechanisms a firewall can use to protect systems, eg: ip address filtering, port filtering, URL filtering and packet inspection, rather than simply saying that it protects a system against intruders.

(*e*)   Backup strategies that the company could adopt in order to ensure a speedy recovery from any future attack include the following:

- Using mirror disks: if a disk is destroyed or corrupted, it can be replaced immediately by its mirror without stopping the system. (1 mark)

- Using backup servers: if a server is compromised it can be replaced immediately by a backup server, with little or no interruption in service. (1 mark)

24.

This question is about Data Transmission, including the TCP/IP protocol suite and Network Interface Cards (NICs).

(a)   The TCP/IP protocol suite consists of two protocols,: TCP (Transmission Control Protocol) and IP (Internet Protocol) which work closely together.

TCP looks after communications between applications software, such as browsers, and network software. (1 mark) It is responsible for breaking data down into IP packets prior to transmission and for reassembling the packets when they arrive at the destination. (1 mark) If one application wants to communicate with another via TCP, it sends a communication request. After a "handshake" has been exchanged by the applications, TCP will initiate a "full-duplex" communication. (1 mark)

IP takes care of communication with other computers. (1 mark) It is responsible for ensuring that packets are sent to the correct destination. (1 mark) IP is a "connectionless" protocol. It reduces the need for network lines as each line can be used for communication between many different computers simultaneously. (1 mark)

(b)   The network interface card (NIC) is responsible converting data from the computer into a form suitable for transmission over the network. (1 mark) Each can be uniquely identified via its 6 byte MAC (Media Access Controller) address. (1 mark)

TOP EXAM TIP

Make sure that you are familiar with the operation of the TCP/IP protocol suite and can distinguish clearly between the functions of TCP and those of IP.

SECTION III

Part C – Multimedia Technology

25.

This questions is about various aspects of Multimedia Technology, including Bluetooth, holographic storage, 3D displays and streaming data.

(a)   Bluetooth technology is used for communication between devices located within 10 metres of one another, eg: between a standalone GPS receiver and a smartphone, (1 mark) or between a PDA and a desktop or laptop PC. (1 mark)

(b)   Holographic storage has an enormous storage capacity as data can be stored through the full depth of the medium, rather than just on the surface. (1 mark) Access speed is very rapid as millions of bits can be written or read in parallel. (1 mark)

(c)   Virtual 3D displays use a virtual-reality headset, which has two monitors showing a different perspective for each eye. (1 mark) Real3D displays illuminate points within a 3D space by means of multi-planar displays or rotating display panels. (1 mark)

(d)   Steaming data can be seen or heard almost immediately, rather than having to wait until the whole fill has downloaded. (1 mark) It requires less memory, since only the data currently being used needs to be stored in memory. (1 mark)

TOP EXAM TIP

Make sure that you are familiar with the newer or less common aspects of multimedia technology, such as Bluetooth, holographic storage and 3D displays.

26.

This question is about various aspects of digital audio.

(a)   MP3 compression is based on the fact that the human ear treats some sounds as less important than others, eg: sounds at very high or very low frequencies cannot be heard at all and if a loud sound and a quiet sound are played at the same time, the quiet sound will be ignored. (1 mark) MP3 compression begins by removing the least important sounds. The remaining data is then compressed using a traditional compression format known as Huffman coding, which is very similar to the compression used in ZIP files. (1 mark) An audio file compressed using MP3 is around a tenth of the size of the original file. (1 mark)

(b) MP3 is described as a "lossy" format because data is discarded during the compression process. A decompressed MP3 file is not identical to the original file, but it should sound the same. (1 mark)

(c) Bit-rate refers to the number of bits used per unit of playback time to represent audio after data compression. The size of an audio file (in bytes) is given by the bit rate (in bit/s) times the length of the recording (in seconds), divided by eight. (1 mark)

(d) The process of ensuring that all the tracks on a digitised album will play at a similar volume level is known as normalisation. (1 mark)

(e) Stereo uses only two channels whereas surround sound uses multiple channels, often six (5.1) or eight (7.1). (1 mark)

(f) If the volume level of an input sound signal is too high for the sound card to deal with the sound will become distorted as clipping will occur. (1 mark)

(g) The name given to the technique of gradually decreasing the volume towards the end of a track is fade-out.

27.

 This question is about various aspects of vector graphics and digital video.

(a) Vector graphics is an object-oriented storage format, meaning that each object in an image is stored separately and can be manipulated separately. (1 mark) Storage is much more efficient than bitmap graphics, because only the instructions required to draw each object are stored, rather than the objects themselves. (1 mark) Vector graphics output can be scaled to match the resolution of the display device without loss of quality. (1 mark) Vector graphics can easily be converted to bitmap format. (1 mark)

(b) Intraframe compression compresses each individual frame, using a lossy technique such as JPEG. (1 mark) Interframe compression Stores only key frames (normally every 10th or 15th frame) and the changes between these and subsequent frames. (1 mark) Further techniques, including reducing bit depth, reducing frame rate, reducing resolution and cropping can be applied to further reduce the size of the final file. (1 mark)

(c) Sound can be incorporated into video files by using AVI (Audio Video Interleave). (1 mark) AVI files can store both audio and video data in a file container that allows synchronous audio-with-video playback. (1 mark)

(d)

  (i) A timeline is a horizontal line along which video clips can be placed to indicate the order and timing they are to be played in. (1 mark)

  (ii) Transition is the movement between video clips. It may involve a simple, straight cut from one clip to the next, fade gently from one scene to the next or use more complex techniques. (1 mark)

  (iii) Sequencing involves moving video clips around in the timeline to alter the order of play. (1 mark)

28.

 This question is about various aspects of bit-mapped graphics.

(a) A scanner uses a moving scan head which can cover the width of the document in a single pass. (1 mark) It contains a linear Charge-Coupled Device (CCD) (1 mark) which consists of a row of linked photo sensors that turn light levels into analogue signals. (1 mark) These analogue signals are fed to Analogue to Digital Convertors (ADCs) where they are converted to digital data representing the image. (1 mark)

(b) $4 \times 3 \times 200 \times 24 = 57600$ bits (1 mark)

$57600/8 = 7200$ bytes (1 mark)

$7200/1024 = 7.032125$ kilobytes (1 mark)

(c) Anti-aliasing is used to smooth out jagged lines or curves or characters by altering the size, shading or alignment of pixels. (1 mark) Dithering is used to create the illusion of non-available colours by using grids of pixels of mixed colours. For example, an orange effect could be created by using a grid of red and yellow pixels. (1 mark)

TOP EXAM TIP

Anti-aliasing and dithering are often confused. Make sure you know the difference between them.

(d) Re-sampling can be used to reduce the file size of bitmapped images. The total number of pixels determines the file size. (1 mark) When you re-sample a bitmap image, the information represented by several pixels in the image is combined to make a single larger pixel. (1 mark)

(e) Advantages: MIDI data files are much smaller than digitised audio files (1 mark) and individual notes can be edited. (1 mark)

Disadvantages: MIDI sound is not as realistic as digitised sound and it cannot deal with vocals. (1 mark)

(f) Instrument: the MIDI instrument being used.
Pitch: the frequency of the sound.
Volume: the loudness or amplitude of the sound.
Duration: the length of the sound, in beats.
Tempo: the number of beats per second.

PRACTICE EXAM D — WORKED ANSWERS

SECTION I

1.

This question is about the two's complement representation of signed binary integers. A binary integer can be converted to two's complement form by changing all the zeroes to ones and vice versa, then adding one.

HINT You may find that drawing up a table like the one shown below helps you answer this type of question. Don't forget that you need to add 1!

128	64	32	16	8	4	2	1	
0	1	1	0	0	1	1	1	**103**
1	0	0	1	1	0	0	0	**Flip 0s and 1s** (1 mark)
						+	1	**Add 1**
1	0	0	1	1	0	0	1	**−103** (1 mark)

2.

This question is about the effect of changing the distribution of bits between the exponent and the mantissa of a floating point number.

The effect of increasing the number of bits assigned to the exponent of a floating point number is to increase the range of numbers that can be represented. (1 mark)

HINT Remember, increasing the size of the exponent increases the range of numbers that can be represented. Increasing the size of the mantissa increases the accuracy or precision with which they can be represented. There is always a trade-off between range and precision as either can only be improved at the expense of the other.

3.

This question is about the functions of the internal components of the Central Processing Unit (CPU).

(i) The Arithmetic and Logical Unit (ALU) is responsible for carrying out arithmetic operations, such as addition, and logical operations, such as comparisons on the data held in the CPU registers. (1 mark)

(ii) The control unit is responsible for coordinating and controlling the actions of the other components of the CPU. (1 mark)

HINT Remember that there are three internal components: the ALU, the control unit and the registers. The registers are storage locations within the CPU which can be used to store instructions, data or addresses temporarily.

4.

This question is about the reset line, which is one of the control lines. The other control lines include the Read, Write, Clock and Interrupt lines. These are sometimes referred to collectively as the Control Bus.

The reset line in the control bus stops the execution of the current program and initiates a reboot. (1 mark)

TOP EXAM TIP

Make sure that you don't confuse the reset line on the control bus with the computer's reset switch.

5.

This question is about solid state memory devices, such as memory cards and pen drives. These are continuing to increase in capacity and decline in price, to the extent that some smaller computers rely solely on solid state memory and have no hard drives.

Solid state memory devices are small and portable (1 mark) and continue to retain stored data after power has been removed. (1 mark)

6.

This question is about the differences between client-server and peer-to-peer networks. Peer-to-operation is only really suitable for small networks.

(*a*) Client-server networks enable critical network functions, such as user authentication, to be centralized on a single machine. (1 mark) They also enable all user files to be stored in a single location, making backup easier. (1 mark)

TOP EXAM TIP

Make sure that you don't confuse peer-to-peer networks with peer-to-peer file-sharing systems.

(*b*) A print server controls printing for all machines attached to the network. (1 mark) A mail server distributes email to all the machines on the network. (1 mark)

7.

This question is about the function of the bootstrap loader.

A bootstrap loader finds the operating system on the hard disk and loads it into memory. (1 mark)

8.

This question is about the differences between trojan horses and computer viruses.

A trojan horse appears to be some useful program which hides malware. Ordinary computer viruses do not pretend to have any useful function. (1 mark) Trojan horses are normally designed to allow a hacker back-door access to a system. Ordinary viruses can have a variety of functions, including corrupting or deleting data. (1 mark)

TOP EXAM TIP

Make sure that you are clear about the differences between computer viruses, trojan horses and worms.

9.

This question is about the roles of the different employees involved in the software development process. These are likely to include a project manager, one or more systems analysts, a client and an independent test group as well as programmers.

The role of a computer programmer is to code, test and implement software (1 mark) in accordance with the supplied design. (1 mark)

10.

This question is about the uses of scripting languages, often provided with applications. They are often used for writing macros to automate tasks or client-side scripts for execution by web browsers.

Scripting languages can be used to customise application packages (1 mark) and to automate repetitive tasks. (1 mark)

11.

This question is about the different data types used in programming languages.

(i)   Surname: String. (1 mark)

(ii)   Gender: Boolean. (1 mark)

(iii)   Number of Dependents: Integer. (1 mark)

(iv)   Height: Floating Point. (1 mark)

TOP EXAM TIP

You should be familiar with the uses of the four main data types:

• String: used to hold strings of characters

• Boolean: used to hold data which can only take one of two values

• Integer: used to hold whole numbers

• Floating point: used to hold numbers which have a fractional point.

One useful way of distinguishing between integers and floating point numbers is to remember that integers are used for counted data, while floating point numbers are used for measured data.

Beware of so-called "numbers" which aren't really numbers at all, eg: telephone number, part number. These would normally be stored as string variables.

12.

This question is about the string handling functions offered by high-level languages.

HINT

The names of string-handling functions and the precise details of their operation can vary between different languages, but almost all languages provide functions for extracting characters from strings and joining strings together.

High-level programming languages normally provide functions for selecting characters from a string (substring), eg: SUBSTR. (1 mark) They also provide functions for joining two strings together (concatenation), eg: CONCAT. (1 mark)

TOP EXAM TIP

Make sure that you are familiar with the string-handling functions available in at least one high-level language.

13.

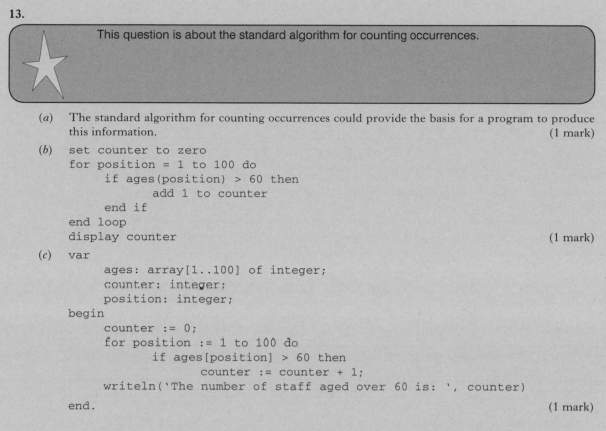

This question is about the standard algorithm for counting occurrences.

(a)   The standard algorithm for counting occurrences could provide the basis for a program to produce this information.   (1 mark)

(b)
```
set counter to zero
for position = 1 to 100 do
      if ages(position) > 60 then
            add 1 to counter
      end if
end loop
display counter                                                        (1 mark)
```

(c)
```
var
      ages: array[1..100] of integer;
      counter: integer;
      position: integer;
begin
      counter := 0;
      for position := 1 to 100 do
            if ages[position] > 60 then
                  counter := counter + 1;
      writeln('The number of staff aged over 60 is: ', counter)
end.                                                                  (1 mark)
```

SECTION II

14.

This question is about the storage requirements for bit-mapped graphics files.

(a)   Bit-mapped images are stored as colour codes for a two-dimensional array of picture elements (pixels). (1 mark)

(b)   The amount of storage required by bit-mapped graphics files can be reduced by decreasing the resolution of the image, ie: the number of dots per inch, (1 mark) or by decreasing the bit-depth of the image, ie: the number of bits used to represent each pixel. (1 mark)

(c)

   (i)   200,000 bytes (1 mark)

   (ii)   400,000 bytes   (1 mark)

15.

The first part of this question is about the functions of the control lines.

(a)   The three main functions of the control lines are the control of reading, writing and timing. The read line is used to initiate a read operation, transferring data from main memory to the CPU. (1 mark) The write line is used to initiate a write operation, transferring data from the CPU to main memory (1 mark) and the clock line sends a series of timing pulses, used to synchronise events. (1 mark)

HINT — The different methods used for measuring computer performance serve different functions. MIPS can be deceptive as the instruction sets on different machines can vary in complexity, FLOPS can provide a useful measure of the efficiency of a machine in calculation-intensive areas, such as scientific or engineering applications. Clock speed is of little relevance unless we know how many bits are processed during each clock cycle. Application-based tests often give the best indication of how a system is likely to perform in real-world situations.

(b)   Methods of measuring the performance of a computer system include MIPS (millions of instructions per second), (1 mark) FLOPS (floating-point operations per second) (1 mark) and clock speed (no. of clock cycles per second). (1 mark)

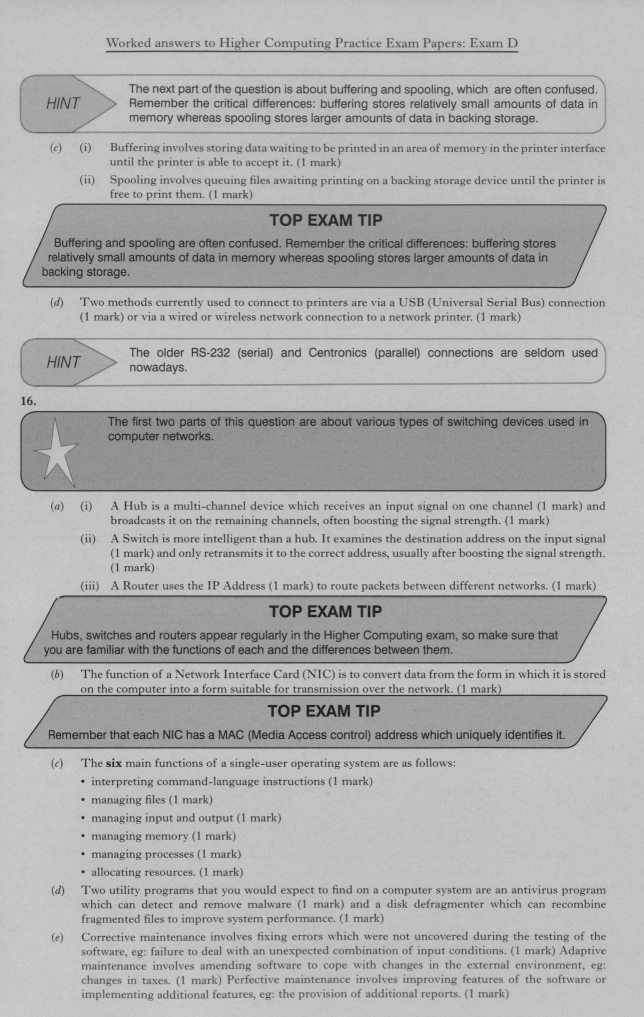

HINT

The next part of the question is about buffering and spooling, which are often confused. Remember the critical differences: buffering stores relatively small amounts of data in memory whereas spooling stores larger amounts of data in backing storage.

(c) (i) Buffering involves storing data waiting to be printed in an area of memory in the printer interface until the printer is able to accept it. (1 mark)

(ii) Spooling involves queuing files awaiting printing on a backing storage device until the printer is free to print them. (1 mark)

TOP EXAM TIP

Buffering and spooling are often confused. Remember the critical differences: buffering stores relatively small amounts of data in memory whereas spooling stores larger amounts of data in backing storage.

(d) Two methods currently used to connect to printers are via a USB (Universal Serial Bus) connection (1 mark) or via a wired or wireless network connection to a network printer. (1 mark)

HINT

The older RS-232 (serial) and Centronics (parallel) connections are seldom used nowadays.

16.

The first two parts of this question are about various types of switching devices used in computer networks.

(a) (i) A Hub is a multi-channel device which receives an input signal on one channel (1 mark) and broadcasts it on the remaining channels, often boosting the signal strength. (1 mark)

(ii) A Switch is more intelligent than a hub. It examines the destination address on the input signal (1 mark) and only retransmits it to the correct address, usually after boosting the signal strength. (1 mark)

(iii) A Router uses the IP Address (1 mark) to route packets between different networks. (1 mark)

TOP EXAM TIP

Hubs, switches and routers appear regularly in the Higher Computing exam, so make sure that you are familiar with the functions of each and the differences between them.

(b) The function of a Network Interface Card (NIC) is to convert data from the form in which it is stored on the computer into a form suitable for transmission over the network. (1 mark)

TOP EXAM TIP

Remember that each NIC has a MAC (Media Access control) address which uniquely identifies it.

(c) The **six** main functions of a single-user operating system are as follows:
- interpreting command-language instructions (1 mark)
- managing files (1 mark)
- managing input and output (1 mark)
- managing memory (1 mark)
- managing processes (1 mark)
- allocating resources. (1 mark)

(d) Two utility programs that you would expect to find on a computer system are an antivirus program which can detect and remove malware (1 mark) and a disk defragmenter which can recombine fragmented files to improve system performance. (1 mark)

(e) Corrective maintenance involves fixing errors which were not uncovered during the testing of the software, eg: failure to deal with an unexpected combination of input conditions. (1 mark) Adaptive maintenance involves amending software to cope with changes in the external environment, eg: changes in taxes. (1 mark) Perfective maintenance involves improving features of the software or implementing additional features, eg: the provision of additional reports. (1 mark)

17.

This question is about program development tools: interpreters and compilers. Many development suites include both an interpreter for use during development and an optimising compiler for producing the final run-time code.

(a) Interpreters are useful during the development stage of a program as they enable the program to be run again quickly. (1 mark) Compilers are more useful for production programs as the translation process only needs to be carried out once. (1 mark)

(b) The main advantages of using a compiler are that compiled code runs faster than interpreted code and the translation process need only be carried out once. (1 mark) The main disadvantages are that the translation process is slow and is inconvenient if a program is subject to frequent changes. (1 mark)

18.

The first part of this question is about the use of the CASE statement (or equivalent) to deal with selections involving more than two alternatives. Programmers generally regard the use of nested if-statements as inelegant, so a CASE statement is preferred.

(a) (i)
```
Select Case DepCode of (1 mark)
Case 10
      Set DepName to "Manufacturing"
Case 11
      Set DepName to "Finance"
Case 12
      Set DepName to "Human Resources"
Case 13
      Set DepName to "Marketing"                      (1 mark)
End Select                                            (1 mark)
```
(ii)
```
var
      depcode: integer;
      depname: string;                                (1 mark)
begin
      case depcode of                                 (1 mark)
      10: depname := 'Manufacturing';
      11: depname := 'Finance';
      12: depname := 'Human Resources';
      13: depname := 'Marketing'
      end                                             (1 mark)
end.
```

TOP EXAM TIP

You should ensure that you are familiar with the use of CASE statements (or equivalent) to handle complex selections. Make sure that you can deal with these in both pseudocode and a high-level language.

(b)

This part of the question is about aspects of program structure, including subprograms, parameter-passing mechanisms and global variables.

(i) A function returns only a single value, which is returned via the function name. (1 mark) A subroutine can return zero or more values which are returned via parameters. (1 mark)

(ii) The department code should be passed to the subprogram as a reference parameter (call by reference) (1 mark) as it does not require to be altered within the subprogram. (1 mark)

(iii) Global variables are not a good idea as their value can be altered anywhere in the program. (1 mark) Every time a programmer considers altering the value of a global variable he/she needs to check that it is not being altered elsewhere in the program. (1 mark)

19.

This question is about using the standard algorithm for finding a minimum value.

(a)
```
set lowest to 0                                                          (1 mark)
{find lowest}
for count = 0 to 99 do                                                   (1 mark)
    if minlevels(count) < lowest then                                    (1 mark)
        set lowest to minlevels(count);                                  (1 mark)
{find lowest years}
Display 'The lowest minimum level occurred in the following years:'      (1 mark)
for count = 0 to 99 do                                                   (1 mark)
    if minlevels[count] = lowest then
        display(1900 + count);                                           (1 mark)
```

(b)
```
var
    minlevels: array[0..99] of integer;
    lowest, count: integer;                                             (1 mark)
begin
    lowest := 0;
    {find lowest}
    for count := 0 to 99 do
        if minlevels[count] < lowest then
            lowest := minlevels[count];                                 (1 mark)
    {find lowest years}
    writeln('The lowest minimum level occurred in the following
    years:');
        for count := 0 to 99 do
            if minlevels[count] = lowest then
                writeln(1900 + count)                                   (1 mark)
end.                                                                     (1 mark)
```

HINT Remember that you need to set the lowest value to zero at the beginning of the algorithm. If you don't do this the implementation will not function correctly in most high-level languages.

SECTION III

Part A – Artificial Intelligence

20.

This question is designed to test your familiarity with some of the more general aspects of Artificial Intelligence.

(a) Originally the emphasis in Artificial Intelligence was on modeling or simulating the activity of the human brain, (1 mark) but it has now moved towards producing systems which exhibit intelligent behaviour. (1 mark)

(b) LISP is a functional programming language, (1 mark) which uses functions to manipulate data structures. (1 mark) Prolog is a logic programming language, (1 mark) used for coding logic-based problems in such a manner that they can be solved by computer. (1 mark)

(c) The following problems are still associated with AI, despite advances in hardware and software:
- There is still no simple, generally-accepted definition of intelligence, never mind artificial intelligence. (1 mark)
- Many AI applications are highly domain-specific and are not easily generalised. (1 mark)
- "Intelligent behaviour" in humans often involves an element of intuition, which is not easily replicated on a computer. (1 mark)
- Many real-world problems are difficult to express in a manner that allows them to be solved by computer. (1 mark)

21.

This question is about some of the key areas of Artificial Intelligence: computer vision, intelligent software and expert systems.

(a) The five stages involved in computer vision are as follows:
- Image acquisition: capturing the image (1 mark)
- Signal processing: converting the image into a format the computer can understand (1 mark)
- Edge-detection: simplifying the picture to produce a wire-frame model (1 mark)
- Object recognition: matching the object with known templates (1 mark)
- Image understanding: making sense of the whole picture (1 mark)

(b) Examples of the use of intelligent software to control devices include:
- Engine management systems for cars (1 mark)
- Autopilot systems for aircraft (1 mark)
- Fridge management systems which monitor stocks of foodstuffs (1 mark)

(c) Expert systems have the following disadvantages:
- They are restricted to a narrow domain (1 mark)
- They lack common sense (1 mark)
- They are difficult to set up and maintain (1 mark)
- They rely on a body of knowledge derived from human experts (1 mark)
- They cannot acquire new knowledge (1 mark)

22.

> This question covers the differences between the breadth-first and depth-first approaches to searching trees.

(a)

(i) A breadth-first search will always find the best solution, ie: the one that takes fewest moves to reach the desired goal, (1 mark) but they are very memory-intensive as the entire tree needs to be stored in memory. (1 mark)

(ii) A depth-first search makes much more efficient use of memory as only the branch currently being searched needs to be stored. (1 mark) However, they can spend a long time on unsuccessful searches and may have to search the whole tree to confirm that the best solution has been found. (1 mark)

(b)

(i) breadth-first: Alloa, Banff, Inverness, California, Forfar, Johnstone, Moscow, Darvel, Elgin, Greenock, Huntly, Keith, Lanark, Newmilns, Ormskirk. (1 mark) (1 mark) (1 mark)

(ii) depth-first: Alloa, Banff, California, Darvel, Elgin, Forfar, Greenock, Huntly, Inverness, Johnstone, Keith, Lanark, Moscow, Newmilns, Ormskirk. (1 mark) (1 mark) (1 mark)

> **TOP EXAM TIP**
>
> Questions of this nature often appear in the Higher Computing exam. You should be able to describe both depth-first and breadth-first searches and trace through the steps.

23.

> The first part of this question is about the construction of a semantic net.

(a)

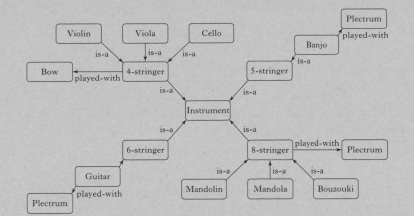

One mark each allocated for:

Instruments as class

4-stringers, 5-stringers, 6-stringers and 8-stringers as sub-classes

Violins, violas, cellos as members of sub-class 4-stringers

Played with bow as attribute of sub-class 4-stringers

Mandolins, mandolas and bouzoukis as members of sub-class 8-stringers

Played with plectrum as attribute of sub-class 8-stringers

Guitar as member of class 6-stringers and banjo as member of class 5-stringers

Played with plectrum as attribute of guitar and banjo

(b)

    (i)   Mandolin

           Mandola

           Bouzouki

    (ii)   Goal instrument(A, long, 5, plectrum).

Match at line 31, first subgoal (1 mark)

neck(A,long) (1 mark)

Match at line 7, A instantiated (1 mark) to bouzouki

Second subgoal strings(bouzouki,5) fails. Backtrack to first subgoal (1 mark)

Match at line 8, A instantiated to g_banjo

Second subgoal strings(g_banjo,5) (1 mark)

Match at line 20, second subgoal succeeds. (1 mark)

Third subgoal playedwith(g_banjo,plectrum) (1 mark)

Match at line 30, third subgoal succeeds. (1 mark)

Goal succeeds, A = g_banjo returned as output

(1 mark)

SECTION III
Part B – Computer Networking

24.

The first part of this question is about IP address classes. You should be aware that there are four different classes of IP addresses, each of which uses a different distribution of the available 32-bits between the network address and the host address. Classes A, B and C are used for different sizes of networks, while Class D is used for broadcasting.

(a)   Class A IP addresses are used for very large networks. (1 mark) 8 bits are allocated to the network address and 24 bits are allocated to the host addresses. (1 mark)

Class B IP addresses are used for large networks. (1 mark) 16 bits are allocated to the network address and 16 bits are allocated to the host addresses. (1 mark)

Class C IP addresses are used for relatively small networks. (1 mark) 24 bits are allocated to the network address and 8 bits are allocated to the host addresses. (1 mark)

Class D IP addresses are used multicast messaging. (1 mark) A class D address is assigned to a group of computers to allow messages to be broadcast to all of them (1 mark)

TOP EXAM TIP

Address classes are no longer in general use, but questions about them can still appear in the Higher Computing exam.

(b)   (i)   Network layer (1 mark)

       (ii)   Transport layer (1 mark)

       (iii) Presentation layer (1 mark)

       (iv) Physical layer (1 mark)

       (v)   Data Link layer (1 mark)

       (vi) Session layer (1 mark)

       (vii) Application layer (1 mark)

HINT   This part of the question is designed to test your familiarity of the OSI Network Model. You should ensure you know the names and functions of all seven layers.

25.

The first two parts of this question deal with Internet access from mobile devices, such as cellphones and PDAs. This is currently the fastest-growing area of internet use. These devices make use of special purpose browsers known as microbrowsers, which reformat the content of web pages for display on a small screen. Some web pages are specifically written for display on mobile devices, using a special language known as WML.

(*a*) Microbrowsers reduce the size of graphics (1 mark) and reformat pages for optimum display on a handheld device, (1 mark) often by means of a proxy server.

(*b*) WML supports only a limited number of styles (1 mark) and has limited support for tables and images. (1 mark) It organises pages into stacks of cards. (1 mark) When the first card is accessed the whole stack is downloaded and cached. (1 mark)

HINT

The next part of the question is about e-commerce, another rapidly expanding area of Internet use. You should be aware of the advantages and disadvantages of e-commerce for both consumers and retailers and of the steps that can be taken to minimise online fraud.

(*c*)

   (i) Retailers can deal directly with customers, cutting out the middleman. (1 mark) They have no need for high-priced retail locations and can operate with fewer staff. (1 mark)

   (ii) Customers can make purchases at any time of the day or night (1 mark) and have access to a far wider range of goods than would be possible in any bricks and mortar store. (1 mark)

(*d*) Teleworking saves employers the cost of expensive office accommodation and saves employees the time and cost of traveling. (1 mark) However, teleworkers can feel socially isolated and employers may not be able to monitor their activities to the same extent as in a traditional workplace. (1 mark)

(*e*) Regulation of Investigatory Powers reduces personal privacy on the internet as it allows the Government and other authorised bodies to:

- Intercept communications (1 mark)
- Acquire communications data, including encrypted data (1 mark)
- Set up covert surveillance (1 mark)

TOP EXAM TIP

The social implications of computer networking, including effects on employment and personal privacy are an area of growing importance. Questions on these topics often appear in the Higher Computing exam.

26.

This question is about various aspects of network security. Good security is crucial for ensuring that users trust networks and are not afraid that their data will be compromised. You should be aware of the importance of Confidentiality, Integrity and Availability and know about some of the ways in which computer networks can be attacked and the steps that can be taken to protect them.

(*a*) The three main requirements for network security are as follows:

- Confidentiality: data must be kept confidential (1 mark)
- Integrity: data must not be lost or corrupted (1 mark)
- Availability: data must be available on demand to authorised users (1 mark)

(*b*) Passive attacks only involve observing what is happening on a network or copying date. (1 mark) Active attacks try to corrupt data or to crash servers. (1 mark)

(*c*) The following techniques can be used by a firewall to prevent intruders from gaining access to a computer network:

- Packet filtering: the firewall can reject incoming packets on the basis of their IP address or domain. (1 mark)
- Port filtering: the firewall can reject packets addressed to specific ports. (1 mark)
- Stateful packet inspection: the firewall can inspect packets for potentially malicious content. (1 mark)

TOP EXAM TIP

Make sure that you can describe in detail how a firewall works, rather than simply saying that it blocks intruders.

(d) Content filtering software can reject harmless content as well as potentially objectionable content. (1 mark) Content filtering relies on accepting someone else's opinion of what constitutes objectionable content.

(e) A walled garden is a method of restricting internet access by only allowing access to specified sites and blocking everything else. (1 mark)

27.

 This question is about various aspects of data transmission. Secure and reliable data transmission underpins all aspects of computer networking, so it is important that you know how it works.

(a) The transmitter and the receiver are synchronised by means of syn characters in synchronous transmission. Data is transferred in blocks. (1 mark) With asynchronous transmission there is no synchronization between sender and receiver. Data is transferred character/by/character, with each character being preceded by a start bit and followed by one or more stop bits. (1 mark)

HINT Packet switching is fundamental to the operation of the Internet. Make sure that you can describe how it works in some detail.

(b) In circuit switching a defined path or circuit, real or virtual, is established between the transmitter and the receiver and all transmission takes place via this path. (1 mark) In packet switching data is split up into packets. Each packet may be transferred between sender and receiver via a different route. Packets are reassembled at the destination. (1 mark)

(c) In CSMA/CD (Carrier Sense Multiple Access / Collision Detect) a system which wishes to transmit checks initially to see if the network is clear. (1 mark) If this is the case, it goes ahead and transmits. However, there is always the possibility that two systems may transmit at the same time, leading to a collision which corrupts the data. (1 mark) If this occurs, the collision is detected and each system waits a different random length of time before attempting retransmission. (1 mark)

TOP EXAM TIP

CSMA/CD crops up frequently in the Higher Computing examination, so make sure that you are thoroughly familiar with its operation.

SECTION III

Part C   Multimedia Technology

28.

 The first two parts of this question are about the various file formats and compression techniques used for bit-mapped graphics.

(a) The Graphics Interchange Format (GIF) uses lossless compression. Each pixel is represented by 8 bits, allowing a maximum of 256 colours. (1 mark) The Joint Photographic Experts Group (JPEG) format uses a variable level of lossy compression. If images are compressed too much there may be a noticeable loss of quality. (1 mark)

(b) Run Length Encoding (RLE) take advantage of the fact that sequences of pixels of the same colour occur frequently in graphic images. These can be represented by a colour code and a number indicating the length of the sequence, rather than by coding each pixel individually. (1 mark) Lempel Ziv Welch (LZW) compression makes use of repeated patterns of bits. These are stored in a table and an index number is allocated to each pattern. The compressed image stores the index numbers rather than the patterns themselves. (1 mark)

TOP EXAM TIP

Make sure that you understand the difference between lossy compression and lossless compression. These terms are used in the context of compressing audio, graphics and video. With lossy compression data is lost during the compression process. When the file is decompressed it is not identical to the original – instead it is recreated in a form which, hopefully, looks/sounds the same as the original. With lossless compression no data is lost and the decompressed file will be identical to the original.

The final part of this question is about the components of a graphics card.